# ATOM-SMASHING POWER OF MIND

ORIGINAL CLASSIC EDITIONS

*Atom-Smashing Power of Mind*

*Narrative of the Life of Frederick Douglass*

*The Art of War*

*The Magic of Believing*

*The Power of Your Subconscious Mind*

*The Prince*

*The Richest Man in Babylon*

*The Science of Getting Rich*

*The Secret of the Ages*

*Think and Grow Rich*

*Think Your Way to Wealth*

# ATOM-SMASHING POWER OF MIND

## CHARLES FILLMORE

WITH INTRODUCTION BY MITCH HOROWITZ

Published 2019 by Gildan Media LLC
aka G&D Media
www.GandDmedia.com

Front cover design by David Rheinhardt of Pyrographx

Interior design by Meghan Day Healey of Story Horse, LLC

Library of Congress Cataloging-in-Publication Data is available upon request

ISBN: 978-1-7225-0222-5

10   9   8   7   6   5   4   3   2   1

# Contents

# Contents

# Introduction to this Edition

## Charles Fillmore:
## The Man Who Never Stood Still

*By Mitch Horowitz*

Spiritual experimenters through the ages, from ancient astrologers and alchemists to contemporary chaos magicians and mind-power mystics, have always availed themselves of the latest technologies of their eras. The New Thought pioneer Charles Fillmore, who founded the vibrant and ongoing Unity movement, was a great example of this.

Born in 1854 on an Indian reservation near St. Cloud, Minnesota, Fillmore and his wife and intellectual partner Myrtle, organized their Kansas City-based Unity ministry into one of the nation's first mass-media ministries. As early as 1907, the Fillmores staffed phone banks with round-the-clock volunteers ready to assist callers with distance prayers. The Unity ministry made early use of radio, targeted mailings, correspondence courses, pamphlets, and well-produced magazines aimed at the large demographic range of Unity's congregants. This included the children's monthly *Wee Wisdom*, which launched the literary career of bestselling novelist Sidney Sheldon when it published the ten-year-old's first poem in 1927.

Up to the eve of his death in 1948, Charles Fillmore remained well versed in the science and technology of the newly dawned atomic era. Fillmore sought to unite the insights of science and practical mysticism in the collection of writings that make up *Atom-Smashing Power of Mind*, which appeared the year after his death.

This 1949 book is one of Fillmore's finest literary efforts. It serves as a powerful and stirring summation of his theology of mind-power metaphysics. At the same time, Fillmore relates the higher abilities of thought to the revolutions in atomic energy that entered public awareness in the years immediately preceding his death. Of this, Fillmore makes a creditable effort, foreseeing future developments in wireless, microwave, and cellular technology. When I consider my failings to stay fully versed in the digital technology of our own era, I am all the more admiring of a frontier boy who grew up not only to establish a major religious denomination but who never stopped learning about the radically changing world around him. Within those changes, Fillmore discovered confirmation of his own universal ideals.

Fillmore's key points and practical insights are now available to you in all of his original verve, spirit, and soaring language with this Original Classic Edition of *Atom-Smashing Power of Mind*. I consider Fillmore's book one of the finest mid-century statements of New Thought philosophy. It is the kind of work that should inspire those of us today who believe that all knowledge—scientific, technological, psychological, medical, and spiritual—ultimately converge. Of this, Charles Fillmore was absolutely certain.

MITCH HOROWITZ is the PEN Award-winning author of books including *Occult America* and *The Miracle Club: How Thoughts Become Reality*. He introduces and abridges G&D Media's Condensed Classics series and is the author of the Napoleon Hill Success Course series, including *The Miracle of a Definite Chief Aim* and *The Power of the Master Mind*.

# Foreword

A great many passages in this book testify to Charles Fillmore's persistent interest in what is popularly called atomic energy and the promise held out by its development of a better world for mankind. As he rejoiced in the scientific achievement of its discovery so he tirelessly devoted his thought to its guidance into the channels of peaceful use. On every occasion he urged those having to do with its development to make sure that this unique form of energy, this great gift of the Father, would not be used to worsen life and destroy mankind.

From another standpoint Charles Fillmore's mind was simply fascinated by the idea of the atom, this infinitesimal particle of substance, and the enormous energy locked up in it. At times he thought of it as the most perfect representation in the manifest world of that divine mental or spiritual energy which pervades all things and which, when properly expressed through the minds of His children, serves so greatly to glorify God. At other times he thought of it as the very essence of this mental or spiritual energy, Spirit-mind itself! The reader will find each one of these standpoints set forth over and over—perhaps vaguely and mystically at times—but ever testifying to the alertness and vitality of Charles Fillmore's mind and his unflagging interest in everything in his world.

As will be readily recognized by Unity readers, the articles appearing as chapters in this book, were originally published in Unity magazine over a period of half a century, one of them going back as far as the year 1898.

In the last paragraph of Chapter 8 the author gives his readers a clear formula for dealing with the problem of the atom:

"The great and most important issue before the people today is the development of man's spiritual mind and through it unity with God. . . . The taproot of all our confusion is our failure to use our mind intelligently. We can only think as God would have us think by adjusting our thoughts to divine ideas. Religion and all that it implies in prayer and recognition of God in idea and manifestation is the one and only way out of the chaos in which we find ourselves. We must therefore begin at once to develop this unity with the Father-Mind by incorporating divine ideas into all that we think and speak."

# Chapter 1

## The Atomic Age

The majority of people have crude or distorted ideas about the character and the location of Spirit. They think that Spirit plays no part in mundane affairs and can be known by a person only after his death.

"But Jesus said, 'God is Spirit'; He also said, 'The kingdom of God is within you.' Science tells us that there is a universal life that animates and sustains all the forms and shapes of the universe. Science has broken into the atom and revealed it to be charged with tremendous energy that may be released and be made to give the inhabitants of the earth powers beyond expression, when its law of expression is discovered.

"Jesus evidently knew about this hidden energy in matter and used His knowledge to perform so-called miracles.

"Our modern scientists say that a single drop of water contains enough latent energy to blow up a ten-story building. This energy, existence of which has been discovered by modern scientists, is the same kind of spiritual energy that was known to Elijah, Elisha, and Jesus, and used by them to perform miracles.

"By the power of his thought Elijah penetrated the atoms and precipitated an abundance of rain. By the same law he increased the widow's oil and meal. This was not a miracle—that is, it was not a divine intervention supplanting natural law—but the exploitation of a law not ordinarily understood. Jesus used the same dynamic power of thought to break the bonds of the atoms composing the few loaves and fishes of a little lad's lunch—and five thousand people were fed.

"Science is discovering the miracle-working dynamics of religion, but science has not yet comprehended the dynamic directive power of man's thought. All so-called miracle workers claim that they do not of themselves produce the marvelous results; that they are only the instruments of a superior entity. It is written in I Kings, 'The jar of meal wasted not, neither did the cruse of oil fail, according to the word of Jehovah, which he spake by Elijah.' Jesus called Jehovah Father. He said, 'The works that I do in my Father's name, these bear witness of me.'

"Jesus did not claim to have the exclusive supernatural power that is usually credited to Him. He had explored the ether energy, which He called the 'kingdom of the heavens'; His understanding was beyond that of the average man, but He knew that other men could do what He did if they would only try. He encouraged His followers to take Him as a center of faith and use the power of thought and word. 'He that believeth on me, the works that I do shall he do also; and greater works than these shall he do.'

"The great modern revival of divine healing is due to the application of the same law that Jesus used. He demanded faith on the part of those whom He healed, and with that faith as the point of mental and spiritual contact He released the latent energy in the atomic structure of His patients and they were restored to life and health.

"Have faith in the power of your mind to penetrate and release the energy that is pent up in the atoms of your body, and you will be astounded at the response. Paralyzed functions anywhere in the body can be restored to action by one's speaking to the spiritual intelligence and life within them. Jesus raised His dead bodies in this way, and Paul says that we can raise our body in the same manner if we have the same spiritual contact.

"What have thought concentration and discovery of the dynamic character of the atom to do with prayer? They have everything to do with prayer, because prayer is the opening of communication between the mind of man and the mind of God. Prayer is the exercise of faith in the presence and power of the unseen God. Supplication, faith, meditation, silence, concentration, are mental attitudes that enter into and form part of prayer. When one understands the spiritual character of God and adjusts himself mentally to the omnipresent God-Mind, he has begun to pray aright.

"Audible prayers are often answered but the most potent are silently uttered in the secret recesses of the soul. Jesus warned against wordy prayers—prayer uttered to be heard of men. He told His disciples not to be like those who pray on the housetop. 'When thou prayest, enter into thine inner chamber, and having shut thy door, pray to thy Father who is in secret, and thy Father who seeth in secret shall recompense thee.'

"The times are ripe for great changes in our estimate of the abiding place and the character of God. The six-day creation of the universe (including man) is described in Genesis is a symbolic story of the work of the higher realms of mind under divine law. It is the privilege of everyone to use his mind abilities in the superrealms, and thereby carry out the prayer formula of Jesus: 'Seek ye first his kingdom, and his righteousness; and all these things shall be added unto you.'"

The foregoing extract is from the "Health and Prosperity" column in Unity for May, 1927. These comments are peculiarly applicable to the present and also to a subject that has been agitating the public mind for some time, the atomic bomb.

Of all the comments on or discussions of the indescribable power of the invisible force released by the atomic bomb none that we have seen mentions its spiritual or mental character. All commentators have written about it as a force external to man to be controlled by mechanical means, with no hint that it is the primal life that animates and interrelates man's mind and body.

The next great achievement of science will be the understanding of the mental and spiritual abilities latent in man through which to develop and release these tremendous electrons, protons, and neutrons secreted in the trillions of cells in the physical organism. Here is involved the secret, as Paul says, "hid for ages and generations . . . which is Christ [superman] in you, the hope of glory." It is through release of these hidden life forces in his organism that man is to achieve immortal life, and in no other way. When we finally understand the facts of life and rid our minds of the delusion that we shall find immortal life after we die, then we shall seek more diligently to awaken the spiritual man within us and strengthen and build up the spiritual domain of our being until, like Jesus, we shall be able to control the atomic energy in our bodies and perform so-called miracles.

The fact is that all life is based upon the interaction between the various electrical units of the universe. Science tells us about these activities in terms of matter and no one understands them, because they are spiritual entities and their realities can only be understood and used wisely by the spiritually developed man. Electricians do not know what electricity is, although they use it constantly. The Christian uses faith and gets marvelous results, the electrician uses electricity and also gets marvelous results, and neither of them knows the real nature of the agent he uses so freely.

The man who called electricity faith doubtless thought that he was making a striking comparison when in fact he was telling a truth, that faith is of the mind and it is the match that starts the fire in the electrons and protons of innate Spirit forces. Faith has its degrees of voltage; the faith of the child and the faith of the most powerful spiritual adept are far apart in their intensity and results. When the trillions of cells in one's body are roused to expectancy by spiritual faith, a positive spiritual contact results and marvelous transformations take place. When Jesus asked His patients, "Believe ye that I am able to do this?" He was making such a contact. Also when He told those to whom He ministered, "Thy faith hath made thee whole," He used the same law. When He turned water into wine and fed five thousand by multiplying a few loaves and fishes, He performed in a masterly and beneficial way what our scientists made possible in a destructive way by releasing through the atomic bomb the pent-up forces of Spirit.

Scientists have invented a machine that records the forces of thought. Every thought expressed by the mind radiates an energy as it passes through the brain cells, and this machine measures the force of these radiations. Sir James Jeans, the eminent British scientist, gives a prophecy of this in one of his books. He says in substance that it may be that the gods determining our fate are our own minds working on our brain cells and through them on the world about us. This will eventually be found to be true, and the discovery of the law of release of the electronic vitality wrapped up in matter will be the greatest revelation of all time.

When we awake to the fact that every breath we draw is releasing this all-potent electronic energy and it is shaping our lives for good or ill, according to our faith, then we shall begin to search for the law that will guide us aright in the use of power.

People the world over were amazed and terrified when they read of the destruction wrought on the cities and people of Japan by two atomic bombs. But do we realize that millions of people are killed every year by atomic force? Doctors tell us that it is the toxin generated in our own bodies that kills us. What produces this destructive force? It must be our own minds, and the remedy must also be in a change in mind. Paul expressed this when he said, "Be ye transformed by the renewing of your mind."

All persons who have dismissed the idea of miracle in the marvelous works of Jesus and His followers, have looked forward to a time when the law they used would be explained, but nearly all expected it to come through spiritual means. But now science has opened up a kingdom having all the possibilities of the kingdom of heaven taught by Jesus. However Jesus said this kingdom is within us and would be exercised constructively through our minds under divine law. The latest discovery of science shows that through the development of the atom a power will be cast right into our midst that will in its physical aspect make the earth equal to our wildest dreams of heaven. Broadcasting stations sending out on the ether light, heat, power, will be established the world over, and every householder will have receiving sets which he can turn on or off at will. The cost will be negligible. Lighter-than-air forms of building material will be discovered and our dwellings will float in the air and be transported from place to place like airplanes. Even the climate of the whole planet may be transformed, destructive forces no longer possible, and peace reign forever. Labor as we now have it will disappear, production will become so easy that a man will in a week raise enough food to last him a year. Everybody will produce abundantly. Everybody will have everything he wants, and no one will slave for wages. Art, science, religion, music, and the finer things of life will be for all the people and those who do not expand their minds to enjoy the finer things of life will be out of step with the times.

Our men of science have found the key that unlocks the door to the physical realm in the kingdom of the heavens, but the spiritual domains are yet to be found and their doors unlocked by the multitude.

There must be a change of mind by the people of the earth before the tremendous uplift to be wrought by atomic energy can become beneficial and permanent. Greed and selfishness will find a way to exploit it to boost their ambition unless they are taught the truth. We should therefore redouble our efforts to show man that the power that rules the world is within him. "Greater is he that is in you than he that is in the world."

# Chapter 2

## The Restorative Power of the Spirit

Not only our Bible but the scriptures of all the nations of the world testify to the existence of an invisible force moving men and nature in their various activities. Not all agree as to the character of this omnipresent force, universal Spirit, but it serves the purpose of being their god under whatever name it may appear. Different nations ostensibly believe in the same scriptures, but they have various concepts of the universal Spirit; some conceive it to be nature and others God. Robert Browning says, "What I call God . . . fools call Nature."

Our Bible plainly teaches that God implanted in man His perfect image and likeness, with executive ability to carry out all the creative plans of the Great Architect. When man arrives at a certain point in spiritual understanding it is his office to co-operate with the God principle in creation. Jesus had reached this point, and He said, "My Father worketh even until now, and I work."

It is possible for man to form states of consciousness that are out of harmony with the God principle, but these do not endure, and through experience man learns to adjust his thought to that of God. "I will be what I will to be" is basic in all creation and it proves itself in the face of human reason and logic. God is free to do as He wills, and He has implanted that same freedom in man. When we understand this ego-forming capacity of man and even of nature, we have the key that unlocks the many mysteries and contradictions that appear in every walk of life.

As the animating life of all things God is a unit, but as the mind that drives this life He is diverse. Every man is king in his own mental domain, and his subjects are his thoughts. When the king of Babylon called Daniel to interpret his dream of the image with the head of gold and feet of clay, the prophet prefaced his interpretation with these words, which contain in essence the kingly authority of every man:

"Thou, O king, art king of kings, unto whom the God of heaven hath given the kingdom, the power, and the strength, and the glory; and wheresoever the children of men dwell, the beasts of the field and the birds of the heavens hath he given into thy hand, and hath made thee to rule over them all: thou art the head of gold."

"Thou art the head of gold" is true of every man, but in his ignorance man thinks he is the feet of clay. This thought of his own inefficiency darkens his mentality, and when the Lord attempts to communicate with him in symbols he has to call upon external sources to explain them.

People in this atomic age civilization ask why God does not reveal Himself now as He did in Bible days. The fact is that God is talking to people everywhere, but they do not understand the message and brush it aside as an idle dream. We need to divest ourselves of the thought that Daniel and Joseph, in fact all the unusually wise men of the Bible, were especially inspired by God, that they were divinely appointed by the Lord to do His work. Everything points to their spiritual insight as the result of work on their part to that end. Daniel as a youth had been taught to worship Jehovah, the one and only God. He restrained the gross appetites of the flesh and thereby made himself receptive to Spirit. "But Daniel purposed in his heart that he would not defile himself with the king's dainties, nor with the wine which he drank." He begged that he and his companion be allowed to eat herbs and drink water, which was granted; and the record says that at the end of even a ten-day test they were in better condition physically than all the youths that ate of the king's dainties, that God gave them knowledge and skill, and that Daniel had "understanding in all visions and dreams."

The body is the instrument of the mind, and the mind looks to the Spirit for its inspiration. A very little observation shows that the purer the mind the greater its capacity to receive and interpret the ideas imparted to it by the Spirit. It does not require a doctor's diagnosis to prove that alcohol confuses the mind and injures the body. The daily toll of automobile accidents proves that drivers with alcohol in their stomachs are trifling with death. Although Paul advises that we eat what is set before us, asking no questions, experience proves that the advice of Daniel leads to better health and clearer thinking. Paul is credited with a giant intellect, but when he advised Timothy to take a little wine for his stomach's sake, we know that he was not inspired by the Spirit of wisdom.

Not only the Scriptures that we look to for authority in our daily living but also the experience of ourselves and our neighbors proves that those who cultivate communion with the Father within become conscious of a guiding light, call it what you will.

Those who scoff at this and say that it is all the work of the imagination are deluding themselves and ignoring a source of instruction and progress that they need above all things. If this sense world were the only world we shall ever know, the attainment of its ambitions might be sufficient for a man of meager outlook and small capacity, but the majority of us see ourselves and the world about us in a process of transformation that will ultimate in conditions here on the earth far superior to those we have imagined for heaven.

"Great is the mystery of godliness," and still greater is the capacity for godliness. When Spirit responds to the seeking mind and begins to reveal the magnitude of that undiscovered country within us, we long for a new language with words describing glories beyond all human comparison. Even our so-called physical body reveals a radiant body (which Jesus referred to as sitting on the throne of His glory) that interlaces the trillions of cells of the organism and burns as brightly as an electric light. Jesus gave His apostles a glimpse of this radiant body when He was transformed before them. "And as he was praying, the fashion of his countenance was altered, and his raiment became white and dazzling."

Jesus was very advanced, and His radiant body was developed in larger degree than that of anyone in our race, but we all have this body, and its development is in proportion to our spiritual culture. In Jesus this body of light glowed "as he was praying." Jesus' body did not go down to corruption, but He, by the intensity of His spiritual devotion, restored every cell to its innate state of atomic light and power. When John was in the state of spiritual devotion Jesus appeared to him, "and his eyes were as a flame of fire; and his feet like unto burnished brass." Jesus lives today in that body of glorified electricity in a kingdom that interpenetrates the earth and its environment. He called it the kingdom of the heavens.

We do not have to look to the many experiences recorded in the Bible of the spiritually illumined to prove the existence of the spiritual supersubstance. People everywhere are discovering it, as they always have in every age and clime. Unless it is put under control of the Christ Mind it takes on psychic and "spooky" expressions, which distort the soul instead of unfolding it under divine law, and drive its victims into our psychopathic sanatoria. However, men will continue to pray, and prayer releases the innate glory of God-Mind, so we must be taught how to establish our identity with the Christ and through it to gain the mastery of the stored-up riches of the man invisible.

The metaphysical literature of our day is very rich with the experiences of those who have found through various channels the existence of the radiant body. One example is Angela Morgan's book "Behold the Angel!" Miss Morgan's writing in this book is a radical departure from her well-known poetical vein. She is specific and to the point in announcing her revelations. She says in the foreword:

> This is a book about the radiant body, the living self of every human being; the immortal structure which is the real self even now in this moment of time. The author, through intense conviction and the validity of recent experience, writes in concrete terms of what to her is as real as flesh, bones, blood, and muscle. There is, behind this "veil of flesh," an actual flamelike structure invisible to our everyday, limited perception. When I say it is "radiant," I mean it literally. . . . It is vividly alive, glorious as the sunrise.

She tells of numerous instances in which she saw hands and feet and other parts of her body lighted or really transformed by the flame invisible.

This convincing confession of Miss Morgan prompts me to tell of my development of the radiant body, during half a century's experience. It began when I was mentally affirming statements of Truth. Just between my eyes, but above, I felt a "thrill" that lasted a few moments, then passed away. I found I could repeat this experience with affirmations. As time went on I could set up this "thrill" at other points in my body and finally it became a continuous current throughout my nervous system. I called it "the Spirit" and found that it was connected with a universal life force whose source was the Christ. As taught in the Bible, we have through wrong thinking and living lost contact with the parent life. Jesus Christ incarnated in the flesh and thereby introduced us by His Word into the original Father life. He said, "If a man keep my word, he shall never taste of death." I have believed that and affirmed His words until they have become organized in my body. Sometimes when I make this claim of Christ life in the body I am asked if I expect to live always in this flesh. My answer is that I realize that the flesh is being broken down every day and its cells transformed into energy and life, and a new body is being formed of a very superior quality. That new body in Christ will be my future habitation.

I have found that the kingdom of God is within man and that we are wasting our time and defeating the work of the Spirit if we look for it anywhere else.

# Chapter 3

## Spiritual Obedience

*I fairly sizzle with zeal and enthusiasm
and spring forth with a mighty faith to do
the things that ought to be done by me.*
—CHARLES FILLMORE

Zeal is the great universal force that impels man to spring forward in a field of endeavor and accomplish the seemingly miraculous. It is the inward fire that urges man onward, regardless of the intellectual mind of caution and conversation.

Paul, the zealot whose name was first Saul, metaphysically is a symbol of varied significance. He was born of Jewish parents in Tarsus, Asia Minor, a city of considerable culture and refinement. He was reared as a Pharisee and educated as a rabbi in schools in Jerusalem. His one conception of salvation did not go beyond that of obtaining it through a perfect performance of the works of the law. But in truth he was a man of deep religious character and worshiped the living God.

He was on his way to Damascus to persecute the disciples of Jesus, no doubt in one instant "breathing threatening and slaughter against the disciples of the Lord" and in the next swearing allegiance to the living God whom he worshiped. "As he journeyed . . . suddenly there shone round about him a light out of heaven: and he fell upon the earth." Because of the great blaze of illumination he was struck temporarily blind.

Thus through the spiritual power of his own mind, apparently by accident, he broke into the ethers where his consciousness was flooded with spiritual light, and he heard the voice of Jesus saying: "Saul, Saul, why persecutest thou me? . . . and when his eyes were opened, he saw nothing; and they led him by the hand, and brought him into Damascus."

This experience illumined, expanded, and enriched his whole being, and eventually led him into his life's work: preaching the gospel of Jesus Christ to the whole Gentile world.

Paul presents a tremendous outpouring of zeal; first on the intellectual plane as champion of the law and the prophets, afterward as a disseminator of the freeing doctrine of the Christ. He was a "chosen vessel" of the Lord, and "not disobedient unto the heavenly vision." Yet on several occasions he allowed his zeal to run away with his better judgment and as a result suffered many things.

Zeal should be tempered with wisdom. It is possible to be so zealously active on the intellectual plane that one's vitality is consumed and there is nothing left for spiritual growth. "Take time to be holy." Never neglect your soul. To grow spiritually you should exercise your zeal in spiritual ways.

As children of God our place is at the right hand of the Father. When man really realizes this, he calls down upon himself the baptism of the Holy Spirit. He soon learns that obedience to Spirit increases his power to control his thoughts and thus make his world conform to the divine standard.

When man is obedient to Spirit he will not suffer burdens. To trust Spirit he must know of its guidance by experience. By those who have not learned the guidance of Spirit, that experience must be acquired. Man is spirit and must find himself before he can communicate with universal Spirit.

Paul had his weak points, but he was a great apostle and made Jesus' doctrine live. No doubt the light of spiritual understanding with which his consciousness was flooded at the time of his conversion carried him a long way in his ministry. His fearlessness was the strong point of his character. To him the gospel came first and the things of the world second. This is what made him a great apostle of the Lord. When will and understanding are joined in consciousness man is equal to any emergency.

Without doubt the secret of Paul's great illumination at the time of his conversion is that in previous lives he had built up a spiritual consciousness, and on his way to Damascus he "stirred up" the gift that was within him. The new race that is now being born on this planet will develop these unused resources of the mind by realization, audible prayer, and thanksgiving and bring to the surface the riches of both the subconscious and the superconscious mind.

Above all other Bible writers Paul emphasizes the importance of the mind in the transformation of character and body. In this respect he struck a note in religion that had been mute up to this time; that is, that spirit and mind are akin and that man is related to God through his thought. Paul sounds again and again in various forms this silent but very essential chord in the unity of God and man and man and his body. All Christian metaphysicians are indebted to him for many quotable Scriptures that fortify their position that the mind is the center of man's world around which, to him, all things revolve.

Spiritual realization changes things. In scientific prayer realization is the high point of attainment. With concentrated spiritual attention man can affirm in faith that God Spirit is present and that he, man, is one with the God presence.

That there is a certain unity also between the mind and the elements, mystics contend, and this is borne out by the power exercised by Jesus when He stilled the wind and stopped the storm.

The question is often asked, Does the race mind affect nature and to what extent? Some geologists surmised that exploding bombs might have been the cause of the Japanese earthquake following World War II. Science cannot verify this surmise, although it does teach the unity of all things.

When the scientific world investigates the so-called miracles of religion and discovers that they are being duplicated continually, the power of mind over matter will be heralded as of great importance to both religion and science.

Prayer gives spiritual poise to the ego, and it brings forth eternal life when spiritually linked with the Christ. "If a man keep my word, he shall never see death."

Jesus understood the realm of divine substance, and it was obedient to His word. He will continue to draw upon this omnipresent source of power and also include us in its life-giving energy if we will abide with Him in the Spirit. When we understand the innate capacity of the mind raised to spiritual dominion we cannot but have an increase of faith equal to doing the works of Jesus, and even greater works, as He promised.

Machines that measure the energy used by the mind acting on the brain cells have already been invented, but there is no account of the brain voltage of a person in prayer. When such measurements have been made we shall know something of the capacity of the mind in its highest range of expression. Jesus also called attention to the power of a group praying with Him. "For where two or three are gathered together in my name, there am I in the midst of them."

The first mention of this dynamic power of the Spirit is found in Acts 1 and 2, when the early followers of Jesus were gathered in the "upper chamber."

They all became spiritual dynamos, as revealed in the Greek word translated "power." These disciples had been with Jesus for over three years, but did not have the inspiration or power that was poured out upon them at this historical gathering, which has ever since been an outstanding example of the marvelous spiritual experiences of those who are of one mind and heart in their group worship of Jesus the Christ. It is recorded that the Spirit came upon them like a wind and sat upon each of them in "tongues . . . of fire."

To one who gains even a meager quickening of the Spirit, Christianity ceases to be a theory; it becomes a demonstrable science of the mind.

We must not anticipate better social and economic conditions until we have better men and women to institute and sustain those conditions.

Jesus said that He was the bread and substance that came down from heaven. When will our civilization begin to realize and appropriate this mighty ocean of substance and life? A finer civilization than now exists has been conceived by many from Plato in his "Republic" to Edward Bellamy in "Looking Backward." But a new and higher civilization will be developed only through the efforts of higher and finer types of men and women. Philosophers and seers have looked forward to a time when this earth would produce superior men and women, but save Jesus none has had the spiritual insight to declare, "Verily I say unto you, This generation shall not pass away, until all these things be accomplished." The Greek word genea, here translated "generation," does not mean a little span of thirty-three years of life, but covers the whole race history in its multitudinous births and deaths, incarnations and reincarnations throughout the millions of years since we began to function in creative Mind. It is out of this race that the new race is to come forth. "Ye are the people." The time is at hand for those who are spiritually ripe to stand forth and realize their spiritual identity. Jesus pointed to this when He said, "Say not ye, There are yet four months, and then cometh the harvest? behold, I say unto you, lift up your eyes, and look on the fields, that they are white already unto harvest."

Prayer, communion with God within, realization, awakens spiritual consciousness and develops true spiritual character. It is the only way to cleanse and perfect the mind and thus permanently heal the body. It is good to get still and think about the inexhaustible resources of infinite Mind; about its presence in all its fullness and its readiness to manifest itself when the law is complied with. Pray with persistence and pray with understanding. Be instant in prayer; and never allow anything to keep you from having your daily quiet hour of communion with God, your own indwelling Father.

One day little Billy and Johnny were climbing around in an old apple tree. Finally they walked out on a limb, and were holding to the boughs above them. But the limb on which they were standing proved to be rotten and gave way, and the boys came tumbling down to the ground. Johnny was hurt and began to cry. But Billy got up with a smile on his face and began brushing the dirt off his clothes.

"Why ain't you hurt?" moaned Johnny. "You was out further on the limb than me."

"I prayed," was the happy reply.

"You didn't have no time to pray," retorted Johnny.

"But it didn't catch me, because I was already prayed up ahead," explained Billy. "So I wasn't scared. I know'd I'd be all right."

"Behold, the man!" Jesus Christ is the type of a new race now forming in the earth. Those who incorporate into consciousness the Christ principles are its members. Sir Francis Galton, the father of eugenics, says: "There is nothing either in the history of domestic animals or in that of evolution to make us doubt that a race of sane men may be formed, who shall be as much superior mentally and morally, as the modern European is to the lowest of the primitive races." It is now being revealed in the renaissance of Christianity, which is pouring its light out upon the world, that this new race is forming in the souls of the spiritual-minded in every nation of the earth. These are "the called" of Scripture, who are being gathered together in spiritual consciousness, and will eventually come forth to rule the world with Jesus Christ. Emerson says: "Great hearts send forth steadily the secret forces that incessantly draw great events, and wherever the mind of man goes, nature will accompany him, no matter what the path."

Let us remember that God is Spirit and all that emanates from God is spiritual, including man. The dominion that God gave to man in the beginning, as recorded in Genesis, is a dominion over spiritual ideas, which are represented in the allegory by material symbols. Hence to exercise his dominion man must understand the metaphysical side of everything in existence. Mind is at the bottom of all life and substance. The mind was not "invented" by the brain, but it has evolved the brain as its most efficient instrument.

Divine Mind is the one and only reality. When we incorporate the ideas that form Divine Mind into our mind and persevere in those ideas, a mighty strength wells up within us. Then we have a foundation for the spiritual body, the body not made with hands, eternal in the heavens. When the spiritual body is established in consciousness, its strength and power is transmitted to the visible body and to all the things that we touch in the world about us.

In the economy of the future man will not be a slave to money. Humanity's daily needs will be met in ways not now thought practical.

In the new economy we shall serve for the joy of serving, and prosperity will flow to us and through us in rippling streams of plenty. The supply and support that love and zeal set in motion are not yet largely used by man, but those who have tested this method are loud in their praise of its efficiency.

# Chapter 4

## I AM or Superconsciousness

Superconsciousness is the goal toward which humanity is working. Regardless of appearances there is an upward trend continually active throughout all creation. The superconsciousness is the realm of divine ideas. Its character is impersonal. It therefore has no personal ambitions; knows no condemnation; but is always pure, innocent, loving, and obedient to the call of God.

The superconsciousness has been perceived by the spiritually wise in every age, but they have not known how to externalize it and make it an abiding state of consciousness. Jesus accomplished this, and His method is worthy of our adoption, because as far as we know, it is the only method that has been successful. It is set forth in the New Testament, and whoever adopts the life of purity and love and power there exemplified in the experiences of Jesus of Nazareth will in due course attain the place that He attained.

Jesus acknowledged Himself to be the Son of God. Living in the superconsciousness calls for nothing less on our part than a definite recognition of ourselves as sons of God right here and now, regardless of appearances to the contrary. We know that we are sons of God; then why not acknowledge it and proceed to take possession of our God heirdom?

That is what Jesus did in the face of the most adverse conditions. Conditions today are not so inertly material as they were in Jesus' time. People now know more about themselves and their relation to God. They are familiar with thought processes and how an idea held in mind will manifest itself in the body and in affairs; hence they take up this problem of spiritual realization under vastly more favorable conditions. An idea must work out just as surely as a mathematical problem, because it is under immutable law. The factors are all in our possession, and the method was demonstrated in one striking instance and is before us. By following the method of Jesus and doing day by day work that comes to us, we shall surely put on Christ as fully and completely as did Jesus of Nazareth.

The method by which Jesus evolved from sense consciousness to God consciousness was, first, the recognition of the spiritual selfhood and a constant affirmation of its supremacy and power. Jesus loved to make the highest statements: "I and the Father are one." "All authority hath been given unto me in heaven and on earth." He made these statements, so we know that at the time He was fully aware of their reality. Secondly, by the power of His word He penetrated deeper into omnipresence and tapped the deepest resources of His mind, whereby He released the light, life, and substance of Spirit, which enabled Him to get the realization that wholly united His consciousness with the Father Mind.

In making His great overcoming Jesus applied the principles of Being scientifically, and He instructed His followers to do as He did. No one can get a copyright on the principles of Truth any more than he can get a corner on the air. Truth is free; it is Spirit, and cannot be kept from the spiritually minded, nor can it be confined within the bounds of any religious organization. In the light of modern science the miracles of the Bible can be rationally explained as Mind acting in an omnipresent spiritual field, which is open to all men who develop spiritually. "Ye who have followed me, in the regeneration when the Son of man shall sit on the throne of his glory, ye also shall sit upon twelve thrones, judging the twelve tribes of Israel."

"He that overcometh, I will give to him to sit down with me in my throne."

Overcoming is a change of mind from error to Truth. The way of overcoming is first to place one's self by faith in the realization of Sonship, and second, to demonstrate it in every thought and act.

The Word is man's I AM. The Holy Spirit is the "outpouring" or activity of the living Word. The work of the Holy Spirit is the executive power of Father (mind) and Son (idea), carrying out the creative plan. It is through the help of the Holy Spirit that man overcomes. The Holy Spirit reveals, helps, and directs in this overcoming. "The

Spirit searcheth all things, yea, the deep things of God." It finally leads man into the light.

The work that the overcomer does for the world is to help establish a new race consciousness, "new heavens and a new earth, wherein dwelleth righteousness." By being true to his highest understanding of Truth the overcomer never swerves to the right nor left for any reason.

As an illustration, a friend of mine who lives in a large American city, an executive of a manufacturing corporation, dotes on standing at a bar with a group of his associates; and after they have all ordered liquor in one form or another, he calls out so everyone can hear, "Buttermilk!"

This has been going on for a number of years. Whenever they undertake to joke him about his seemingly tame choice he is overjoyed. He feels he is testifying for the Lord and is thankful just for the opportunity. However he says that first one and then another of his friends has come to him privately and asked him how he has the nerve always to turn down the drinks. He tells them he stands in the strength of the Lord and that it is no problem at all for him. They usually admit they wish they had as much backbone as he. This gives him the opportunity to present a word for the practical use of Truth.

The mind of man is built on Truth, and the clearer man's understanding of Truth is the more substantial his mind becomes. It is through progressive, step-by-step spiritual unfoldment that Truth is demonstrated.

The truths of Being are scientific, and undoubtedly Jesus understood and taught the properties of the cosmic ether under the name of "the kingdom of the heavens."

Science rightly understood is of inestimable value to religion, and Christianity in order to become the world power that its founder envisioned, must stress the unfoldment of the spiritual mind in man in order that he may do the mighty works promised by Jesus.

When Jesus went up into the mount to pray He was transfigured before His apostles Peter, James, and John. True prayer brings about an exalted radiation of energy, and when it is accompanied by faith, judgment, and love, the word of Truth bursts forth in a stream of light that, when held in mind, illumines, uplifts, and glorifies.

Jesus recognized Mind in everything and called it "Father." He knew that there is a faith center in each atom of so-called matter and that faith in man can move upon the faith center in so-called matter and can remove mountains.

He developed spiritual faith in His own mind, which moved upon the cells of His body and released the power He used in His resurrection and ascension.

We cannot separate Jesus Christ from God or tell where man leaves off and God begins in Him. To say that we are men as Jesus Christ was a man is not exactly true, because He had dropped that personal consciousness by which we separate ourselves from our true God self. He became consciously one with the absolute principle of Being. He proved in His resurrection and ascension that He had no consciousness separate from that of Being, therefore He really was this Being to all intents and purposes.

Yet He attained no more than what is expected of every one of us. "That they may be one, even as we are" was His prayer.

This is all accomplished through the externalization of the superconsciousness, which is omnipresent and ever ready to manifest itself through us as it did through Jesus. Let "Christ be formed in you."

In Acts 1:8 Jesus said: "But ye shall receive power, when the Holy Spirit is come upon you."

Through the Holy Spirit, man not only has power to keep the words of Jesus but also to do the works that He did, even "greater works."

Modern science tells us that in the trillions of cells in our body there are imprisoned electronic energies beyond all possibility of estimate; that a single teardrop has within its atoms dynamic force enough to blow up a six-story building. Man is coming into an understanding of how to release these mighty powers and use them in regenerating soul and body.

Jesus taught that the realities of God are capable of expression here in this world and that man within himself has God capacity and power.

Jesus was crucified because He claimed to be the Son of God. Yet the Scriptures, which the Pharisees worshiped, had this bold proclamation, which Jesus quoted to them from Psalms 82:

*I said, Ye are gods,*
*And all of you sons of the Most High."*

Jesus differed from other men in that He proved by His works that He was the Son of God, while the average man is still striving to attain that excellency.

The reports by His followers of what He taught clearly point to two subjects that He loved to discourse upon. The first was the Son of God: He was the Son of God. Secondly: We might all become as He was and demonstrate our dominion by following Him in the regeneration.

In order to follow Jesus in the regeneration we must become better acquainted with the various phases of mind and how they function in and through the body.

He who has caught the significance of man, and who and what man is, never allows himself to accept any erroneous conclusions as to his final destiny. He does however know there is a way provided by which he can not only free himself from the claims of materiality but also by his efforts open the way for many others to do likewise. No person ever demonstrated his God-given powers in even a small way but what he helped others to do the same.

Preaching is good, but precept is better. "I, if I be lifted up from the earth, will draw all men unto myself."

In Isaiah 65:17 we read: "Behold, I create new heavens [ideals] and a new earth [manifestation]; and the former things shall not be remembered, nor come into mind."

The body that is formed in regeneration absorbs the substance of the body of flesh, and makes out of it a new body in divine order, under the law of the Christ Mind. In this process the physical body dies so that the Christ body may live; but the spiritual ego, the I AM, remains consciously active throughout the process of development that Paul referred to when he said: "I die daily."

In spiritual understanding we know that all the forces in the body are directed by thought and that they work in a constructive or a destructive way, according to the character of the thought. Medicine, massage, and all the material means accomplish but incomplete, unsatisfactory, temporary results, because they work only from the outside and do not touch the inner springs that control the forces. The springs can only be touched by thought. There must be a unity between the mind of man and Divine Mind so that ideas and thoughts that work constructively unto eternal life may be quickened in the mind and organism of man.

Jesus unfolded the consciousness of the Absolute.

Through the quickening of the Spirit we are loosed from all limiting ideas and are set free in the Christ consciousness or realization of the Absolute. The consciousness of the Lord Jesus Christ is of limitless life, strength, power, wisdom, love, and substance that are everywhere present, always present.

We are told in John that the world could not contain the books that would be written if all the things that Jesus did were put into writing. But enough is given in the story of His life and in the writings of the apostles concerning Him to bear witness to that which is daily being revealed in this day of fulfillment. Those who are consecrated to Truth and fully resolved to follow Jesus all the way are spiritualizing the whole man, including the body, which is being redeemed from corruption. Those who are living as Jesus lived are becoming like Him. "God is not the God of the dead, but of the living."

Resurrection takes place in people who are alive. One does not go into the grave to be resurrected and to enter the heavenly state of those raised in Christ.

# Chapter 5

## The Day of Judgment

As we come to a realization of an entirely different consciousness new relations are set up that it is sometimes difficult to explain to one who believes in time and space.

In the Bible description of the "day of judgment" the Son of man has always been represented as Jesus Christ, who is to be surrounded by angels and sit on a throne passing judgment after death upon the just and the unjust. But we understand the Son of man to be the spiritual man, that which is ideal, unlimited, and divine. We come into entirely different relations when we affirm, "I am a divine being." When we affirm this we begin to pass judgment. We are the same man, but divine ideas (angels) must come into our consciousness. Then we begin to judge and know that our everyday thoughts are different from our divine, ideal thoughts. We judge between our good thoughts and our evil thoughts, our unlimited and our limited thoughts.

It is said we are to be judged after death according to deeds done in the body, which are kept on record like books that are balanced; and if the balance is found to be in our favor we go up, and if against us we go down. But if we are spiritual now—divine—this spiritual part has dominion, and we begin to exercise this dominion. The moment we catch sight of this we begin to judge. We begin to put the thoughts that are good on the right and the others on the left. All our ideas of the attributes of our divine self we put on the right hand of power, while the thoughts of disease, death, limitation and lack we put on the left—denied, cut off.

This is not to occur after death. It is to begin right now!

We don't say that all is evil; that would be mental suicide. We just say it is a "goat thought." We do not kill it but transform it.

After separating our innocent sheep thoughts, we begin to have fine, high, discriminating judgment.

Then the Son of man has come in His glory, surrounded by His angels (ideas). We know that He is limitless. "I am now a son of God," we say. "I am divine." These angels (ideas) take their places on the throne with the Son of man and judgment begins immediately.

Then today is the day of judgment!

We may have the perception and may see the angels (ideas) but we have not passed judgment. We do not judge until we begin to deny and affirm. Judgment commences the moment you accept the truth of your divine sonship.

"Then shall the King say to them on his right hand, Come, ye blessed of my Father, inherit the kingdom prepared for you from the foundation of the world."

Who is the king? The center of consciousness, the I AM, and the I AM has power to just the extent you have the courage to assert your power. We must all step forth and assert, "All authority hath been given unto me in heaven and on earth." If the central spark is like the divine, then we have all power.

We are here as the king, and we say to our true thoughts (angels), "Come . . . inherit the kingdom prepared for you from the foundation of the world." Then all is ours. There is no limit. We ask what we will and it is done unto us. All good that we can conceive of is now ours. Is there evidence of the oak in the acorn? No! But there is a pattern of an oak there, and this pattern or image is what makes the tree. The image in mind makes the condition.

Now is the time to plant the seed thought of the conditions we desire by saying, "Come my good thoughts, let us inherit our kingdom."

We do not fear anything, for we have separated our sheep from the goats; we have set our true thoughts on the right and have denied our error thoughts any power whatever.

"I was hungry, and ye gave me to eat; I was thirsty, and ye gave me drink; I was a stranger, and ye took me in; naked, and ye clothed me; I was sick, and ye visited me; I was in prison, and ye came unto me."

We understand that our good thoughts always minister to us in days of despondency and discouragement. We rest in the thought that we have done a good deed in such and such an instance or that we have been good at such and such a time. These are the thoughts that minister to us. These thoughts are not conscious; but they are laying the foundation for the coming of the Lord, so they say: "When saw we thee hungry, and fed thee? or thirsty, and gave thee drink? When saw we thee a stranger, and took thee in? or naked, and clothed thee? Or when saw we thee sick, or in prison, and came unto thee?"

Every thought of goodness makes a place, a form, and sets up a friendly habit in the mind that is permanent and that in your time of need ministers to you. You are glad to accept this ministry, for you have done good because the Spirit of good is working through you. Thus you reap the benefit of all the good you have ever done or thought. Your thoughts give back results of the same nature as themselves. If in the silence you have earnestly held to the pure and good you have built in you a place for the pure and good. Every true thought has made a place in your mind and when you are about to judge you will recognize it, although you did not realize it at the time you sent it forth.

We are carried along by these thoughts until we reach the consciousness of our I AM power. We do not know we are building ourselves, our environment, our world, until we reach this consciousness.

Then judgment of our world begins and is passed on our thought creations. Suppose we have tried to cast the beam out of our eye so that we might help our brother. This act will answer in our judgment day, "I was that 'least' one."

Come into the kingdom of mind. Here everything that is in Principle is yours.

These error thoughts and misconceptions of Truth are only age-lasting, not everlasting.

Everything, all good, is to be gathered up, and everything is good at its center. The essence of your body is good and of true substance. When you sift your consciousness of all but the real and true, the body becomes full of light.

The diamond owes its brilliance to the perfect arrangement of the innumerable little prisms within it, each of which refracts the light of the other. Man's body is made up of centers of consciousness—of light—and if arranged so they radiate the light within you, you will shine like the diamond. All things are in the consciousness and you have to learn to separate the erroneous from the true, darkness from light. The I AM must separate the sheep from the goats. This sifting begins right now and goes on until the perfect child of God is manifest and you are fully rounded out in all your Godlike attributes.

# Chapter 6

## Thou Shalt Decree a Thing

*As imagination bodies forth*
*The forms of things unknown, the poet's pen*
*Turns them to shapes, and gives to airy nothing*
*A local habitation and a name.*

—SHAKESPEARE

To decree with assurance is to establish and fix an ideal in substance. The force behind the decree is invisible, like a promise to be fulfilled at a future time; but it binds with its invisible chains the one who makes it. We have only a slight conception of the strength of the intangible. We compare and measure strength by some strong element in nature. We say "strong as steel." But a very little thought will convince us that mental affirmations are far stronger than the strongest visible thing in the world. The reason for this is that visible things lack livingness. They are not linked with energy and intelligence as are words. Words charged with power and intelligence increase with use, while material things decrease.

It is not necessary to call the attention of metaphysicians to the fact that all visible things had their origin in the invisible. The visible is what remains of an idea that has gradually lost its energy. Scientists say that this so-called solid earth under our feet was once radiant substance. Nothing is really "solid" but the atomic energy latent in everything. They tell us that it takes some six billion years for uranium to disintegrate and become lead, and this rate of disintegration has helped scientists determine the age of the earth as about two billion years.

Since nothing is lost in the many transformations that occur in nature, what becomes of the energy that is being released in the disintegration that is going on in our earth? The answer is that a new earth is being formed in which matter will be replaced by atomic energy. This process of refining matter into radiant substance is taking place not only in the natural world but in our bodies also. In fact the speed with which the transformation takes place depends on the character of the thoughts that we project into our brains and through them into our bodies and the world about us. This is why we should spiritualize our thoughts and refine the food we eat to correspond. The press announces a great shortage of meat all over the world, with alarming predictions of malnutrition and race deterioration. Instead of a calamity this meat shortage will prove a blessing. New and better foods will be found to replace the corrupt flesh with which people have been stuffing their stomachs. The call for stimulants that the fermenting mess produces in digestion will diminish, and a purer, sweeter body and saner mind will follow. The peoples of Europe, forced by the economic conditions brought about by wars, are adopting a simpler diet, with better health; so says the public press. Thus what seems calamity turns out to be a source of joy.

At the present writing there is a housing shortage everywhere and the lack of materials and competent labor indicate that several years will elapse before the need is met. This is counted a calamity; but is it? The inventive genius of man is planning houses of glass and other materials that will be much less expensive—more durable and in every respect superior to the present homes. When man gets his ingenious mind into action he always meets every emergency with something better. These many examples of the power of man's mind should make us pause when we are tempted to consider any situation disastrous or nearly so. Every adverse situation can be used as a spur to urge one to greater exertion and the ultimate attainment of some ideal that has lain dormant in the subconsciousness. The pessimist moans, "I could make a better world than this." The optimist sings, "Go to it; that's what God put you here for."

People everywhere on earth are now realizing as never before that the well-being of this world rests with its inhabitants. It is no longer a religious dogma or a philosophical theory that the destiny of the race is in the hands of man. God has given all things to us to use as we shall determine. We can use the atomic energy to destroy or construct as we decree. "Behold, I set before you the way of life and the way of death."

The dominion and authority God gave to His image-and-likeness man has assumed such reality that even the most trivial person can understand it and tremble at the prospect of what might come to pass if that dominion were used by vicious men.

Those who have recklessly gone on living without seeking the wisdom of the source of life are now asking what shall be done to save us from the insanity that would destroy our world.

The one and only answer, of course, is that the moral and spiritual standard of the race must be raised the world over as the one and only ultimate source of safety. This means that every person must begin on himself and, as it dawns, let the light shine by imparting it to others. If this method were followed universally the millennium would be upon us in a marvelously short time.

This is not a religious question but a matter of life or death; not a question of hell after death but of survival here and now of everybody and everything one holds dear. There are Hitlers still alive and others reincarnating. They must all be educated morally and taught the nearness of the spiritual man and the necessity of his incorporation into the consciousness of the natural man before permanent life can be established in the individual. This work is to be done for our race right here on this planet, and for this reason we who love the Lord and greatly desire that His law be fulfilled are calling on all people to make haste and accept the abundant life and light that He so freely offers.

The Bible records many instances where marvelous results followed the observance of religious rites in which trumpets took a leading part. The priests under Moses were ordered to blow trumpets before the Ark; Gideon and his three hundred overcame a large army of Midianites by flashing lights, shouting, and blowing trumpets; the walls of Jericho fell as the result of trumpet and voice vibrations. Isaiah says: "And it shall come to pass in that day, that a great trumpet shall be blown; and they shall come that were ready to perish in the land of Assyria [the psychic realm], and they that were outcasts in the land of Egypt [materialism]; aud they shall worship Jehovah in the holy mountain in Jerusalem [spirituality]."

The trumpet sets up sharp vibrations in the ether, which cause disintegration when they impinge upon an object in the mental or material realms. These realms Isaiah symbolically refers to as Assyria and Egypt. Trained metaphysicians produce like results through the spiritual word, uttered audibly or silently or both. It is in this field of Spirit that Unity people are destined to do a great work in helping to educate people everywhere. By declaring and decreeing spiritually the words of Jesus and Jehovah we send into the ether a spiritual force that shatters the fixed states of consciousness holding millions in evil ways. In this way the doors of mental prisons will be opened to multitudes of sin-bound souls. Anyone who has faith in Spirit and the power of the word spoken in faith can send it forth, and like the radio oscillation, it will be picked up by receptive minds everywhere.

"Let your light shine before men; that they may see your good works, and glorify your Father who is in heaven."

# Chapter 7

## Thinking in the Fourth Dimension

Scientists tell us that the discoveries that their efforts are revealing convince them that they are just on the verge of stupendous truths. Christianity spiritually interpreted shows that Jesus understood the deeper things of God's universe. He understood exactly what the conditions were on the invisible side of life, which is termed in His teaching the "kingdom of God" or the "kingdom of the heavens." We are trying to connect His teaching with modern science in order to show the parallel; but as He said in Mark 4:23, "if any man hath ears to hear, let him hear." This means that we must develop a capacity for understanding in terms of the atomic structure of the universe.

Unless we have this spiritual capacity we do not understand. We think we have ears, but they are attuned to materiality. They do not get the radiations from the supermind, the Christ Mind. Physiology working with psychology is demonstrating that hearing and seeing can be developed in every cell in the body, independent of ears and eyes. We hear and see with our minds working through our bodies. This being true, the capacity to hear may extend beyond the physical ear into the spiritual ethers, and we should be able to hear the voice of God. This extension of hearing is what Jesus taught. "If any man hath ears to hear, let him hear."

Then we are told that we must "take heed" what we hear. Many of us have found that as we develop this inner, spiritual hearing, we hear voices sometimes that do not tell the truth. These deceptive voices can be hushed by affirming the presence and power of the Lord Jesus Christ.

As you unfold your spiritual nature, you will find that it has the same capacity for receiving vibrations of sound as your outer, physical ear has. You do not give attention to all that you hear in the external; you discriminate as you listen. So in the development of this inner, spiritual ear take heed what you hear: discriminate.

Jesus said, "For he that hath, to him shall be given: and he that hath not, from him shall be taken away even that which he hath." How can what a man has not be taken away? We believe in our mortal consciousness that we have attained a great deal, but if we have not this inner, spiritual consciousness of reality our possessions are impermanent. Then we must be careful what we accumulate in our consciousness, because "he that hath, to him shall be given." The more spiritual Truth you pile up in your mind, the more you have of reality, and the larger is your capacity for the unlimited; but if you have nothing of a spiritual character, what little you have of intellectual attainment will eventually be taken away from you.

The kingdom of the heavens, the new dimension of mind and energy that is being unfolded today in the spiritual ethers by the discoveries of the scientists, should not be divorced from the kingdom of heaven taught by Jesus. Jesus taught in parables because His listeners were not trained in science.

We know that the kingdom of the heavens or kingdom of God is not a place in the skies but an ideal state in creative mind, ready to be ushered into the minds of men.

We have thought that this kingdom of God was to be introduced into the world in a miraculous way. At the very beginning of His ministry Jesus announced, "The time is fulfilled, and the kingdom of God is at hand"; but it did not then appear. He said, "The kingdom of God cometh not with observation." Its source is not in outer things; it comes from sources within man. So we know that we must develop spiritual understanding and spiritual power in some respects exceeding that of Jesus. "He that believeth on me, the works that I do shall he do also; and greater." Man is the outpicturing of the infinite and creative Mind, and all the capacity of this great Mind is his by inheritance.

Jesus taught that man is the light of God. Without man God should be deaf and dumb and blind. Did you ever think that you are God's ears and God's mouth and God's eyes? You have doubtless heard these statements before, but you have taken them metaphorically; but it is true that man is God, formulated.

God is Spirit, it is plainly taught, and the omnipotent, omnipresent essence from which all things proceed. Both science and religion agree on the fundamental fact that God is the source of all creation. Just how God puts Himself into His creation is not so universally understood or accepted. But Paul says that God is in us all and through us all and above us all; that is, God saturates us. God as Spirit is the ether or soil in which we grow as human plants.

Jesus compared this soil of God to the soil necessary to the vegetable kingdom, in which seed is cast and springs up and grows and unfolds by a series of orderly stages: "first the blade, then the ear, then the full grain in the ear." This seed is the God word, and it is tremendously prolific, much more so than any material seed.

When man points his mind toward God and allows his zeal to run in a single channel, he may become God-intoxicated. Peter the Hermit became intoxicated with the idea that God wanted Jerusalem rescued from Moslem rule, and he rode up and down Europe on his little mule shouting, "God wills it." His fanatical zeal started the Crusades that rolled from Europe to Palestine for nearly two hundred years.

When we recognize that great teachers and leaders of the race have really developed and expressed a superconsciousness that is potential in all persons, we have raised the hopes and the capacities of men from the human to the divine. These scientific discoveries are proving that

God is impartial and absolutely just in all His relations with humanity. When the natural world is scientifically and universally revealed, a great school of instruction in soul unfoldment will be established right here in our midst, and its results will be beyond all our present imaginings.

The mysteries of the supermind have always been considered the property of certain schools of occultists and mystics who were cautious about giving their truths to the masses for fear that in their ignorance these might misuse them. But now the doors are thrown wide open, and whosoever will may enter in.

Our attention in this day is being largely called to the revolution that is taking place in the economic world, but a revolution of even greater worth is taking place in the mental and spiritual worlds. A large and growing school of metaphysicians has made its advent in this generation, and it is radically changing the public mind toward religion. In other words, we are developing spiritual understanding, and this means that religion and its sources in tradition and in man are being inquired into and its principles applied in the development of a new cosmic mind for the whole human family. So we need a larger realization of the importance of man and the importance of every one of us in manifesting the God who is Spirit.

We have thought that the burden rested on God alone and that we were merely puppets in His hands; but Jesus taught otherwise, and our science proves that man dominates nature when he affirms his mental supremacy. We are told that today we have invented machines that can produce faster than we yet know how to use, that our markets may be glutted with the products of these mechanical inventions, and that the products may become so cheap that those who produce them will come to want. We have wished that everything we touched might turn to gold; it has come to pass and we are paralyzed by the pressure of the stuff we have piled up in our ingenuity and selfishness. We cannot eat it ourselves, and our greed makes us fearful that we shall lose all of it if we pass it out freely to others.

So the great need of the whole human family is to know this one supreme law of God as Spirit manifesting itself in the mind of man. It is then necessary that we understand our own importance as God manifestations. We should understand that we are not separate nor insignificant but the vital, important, integral parts of a mighty whole. Jesus realized the importance of the superman as a thinking power expressing God-Mind when He said, "No one cometh unto the Father, but by me."

We have thought that we were to accept Jesus as our Saviour, that He made propitiation for our sins, and that that was what He meant when He said we could not reach the Father except through Him. We have thought that He meant His personality and His great sacrifice; and we now have to admit that in its deeper, spiritual significance this is in a measure true. But in a more personal and intimate way we are vitally and spiritually intersphered with the Christ Mind in God, and we cannot measure up to and express our divinity unless we accept Jesus' standard of the importance of man and the necessity of man in the great creative scheme of life.

All persons in rare moments catch glimpses of this creative plan as a whole, and of man's importance in its beauty and perfection.

But this subject is so deep and so far-reaching that it can be realized in small degree only by those who have developed spiritual sight and feeling, and practice thinking in the fourth dimension, or kingdom of God.

# Chapter 8

## Is This God's World?

Why doesn't God do something about it?" This oft-repeated query, uttered by the skeptical and unbelieving, is heard day in and day out. Imitating the skeptics, Christian believers everywhere are looking to God for all kinds of reforms in every department of manifest life and also are charging Him with death and destruction the world over.

One who thinks logically and according to sound reason wonders at the contradictions set up by these various queries and desires.

Is God responsible for all that occurs on this earth, and if not all, how much of it?

The Bible states that God created the earth and all its creatures, and last of all man, to whom He gave dominion over everything. Observation and experience prove that man is gaining dominion over nature wherever he applies himself to that end. But so much remains to be gained, and he is so small physically that man counts himself a pygmy instead of the mental giant that he is.

All the real mastery that man attains in the world has its roots in his mind, and when he opens up the mental realm in his being there are no unattainables. If the conquests of the air achieved in the last quarter of a century had been prophesied the prophets would have been pronounced crazy. The fact is that no one thinking in the old mind realm can have any conception of the transformation of sound waves into electromagnetic waves and back again into words and messages of intelligence. Edison admitted that his discovery of the phonograph was an accident and that he never fully understood how mechanical vibrations could be recorded and be reproduced in all forms of intelligent communication.

Reasoning in terms of matter, no one can understand how words and music and pictures can be carried over long distances through space without conflict and then be reproduced by a mechanical device with perfection and accuracy.

Now that man has broken away from his limited visualizations and mentally grasped the unhampered ideas of the supermind, he is growing grandly bold and his technical pioneers are telling him that the achievements of yesterday are as nothing compared to those of tomorrow. For example, an article by Harland Manchester condensed in the Reader's Digest from Scientific American tells of the "micro-waves" that are slated for a more spectacular career in the realm of the unbelievable than anything that has preceded them. This article describes in detail some of the marvels that will evolve out of the utilization of microwaves, among which may be mentioned "private phone calls by the hundreds of thousands sent simultaneously over the same wave band without wires, poles or cables. Towns where each citizen has his own radio frequency, over which he can get voice, music, and television, and call any phone in the country by dialing. Complete abolition of static and interference from electrical devices and from other stations. A hundred times as much 'space on the air' as we now have in the commercial radio band. A high-definition and color television network to cover the country. And, perhaps most important of all, a nation-wide radar network, geared to television, to regulate all air traffic and furnish instantaneous visual weather reports to airfields throughout the land."

Add to this the marvels promised by the appliers of atomic energy and you have an array of miracles unequaled in all the bibles of all the nations of the world.

It is admitted by those who are most familiar with the dynamic power of these newly discovered forces that we do not yet know how to protect our body cells from the destructiveness of their vibrations. Very thick concrete walls are required to protect those who experiment with atomic forces. One scientist says that the forces released from the bombs that were used on the Japanese cities in 1945 may affect those who were subjected to them and their descendants for a thousand years. Experimentation proves that we have tapped a kingdom that we do not know how to handle safely.

It is quite obvious that these forces, if they could be utilized, would vastly improve our standard of living and that they were planned for us by creative Mind. If we cannot control them, why did God allow us to discover them? And now that we are turning them loose in space all about us, what are we going to do about it? Also how do we reconcile this situation with the observation of the Psalmist:

> "*Thou makest him to have dominion over the works*
> *of thy hands;*
> *Thou hast put all things under his feet.*"

The fact is that we have reached a point in race evolution where we are forced to give attention to the refinement of the body. Our religion has too long taught that the body is dust and ashes and that it is its destiny to die and be left to the worms. The deterioration of the body cells must be arrested and a new and more powerful life force injected into the physical organism. This is plainly part of the teaching of Jesus. He said, "I came that they may have life, and may have it abundantly." He told his followers that when they went to that upper room in Jerusalem they would receive the baptism of the Holy Spirit with power. The original Greek says that they would receive dynamic energy. All baptisms with Spirit impart vitalizing life to the recipient, and the joy of quickened vitality should be felt and retained as part of the physical regeneration.

The divine unction imparted by spiritual baptism also contains all the healing forces of X rays, ultraviolet rays, sunshine, and in fact all the radiant restorative forces now so widely used as healing agents. But the energy imparted by Spirit is so tempered that it never injures but always heals. That this is not true of the shocks given by mechanical generators is evidenced by the scars they often leave. A prayer treatment by an experienced spiritual healer is a baptism, with power proportioned to the spiritual understanding of the healer. The lowest method of imparting spiritual baptism is by the laying on of hands and prayer. The highest is realizing the Holy Spirit presence and its expression through the power of the word. Jesus began His ministry by doing the former, but at the end He sent His word and healed by means of it.

God created the fundamental ideas culminating in the idea of ideal man. This ideal man has power to mold God's creation into any manifestation he may choose. If he consults the Father and projects his thoughts in accordance with the law, perfect manifestation follows. As Jesus said, "My Father worketh even until now, and I work."

One who understands this relation of man to his creator can assert with confidence that this is man's world and always will be. By right thinking man can have the co-operation of God in producing manifestations and thereby can set up the kingdom of God in the earth; or he can ignore God and attempt to form a world and govern it without divine aid. We are now living in a civilization dominated by human thought, and confusion is the result.

How many ages and aeons have passed since man lost contact with God no one can tell. We have about six thousand years of history and no heavenly conditions are recorded. Caves and sand drifts reveal the remains of man in combat with the gorilla for half a million years, with man himself sunk almost to the level of the monkey. When man dropped out of the ethers and became one of the primates mortal understanding has not yet discerned, but the distortions in the earth and all nature bear evidence of a terrible shock.

We know that our home is not altogether on the earth but also in the air, over which we must gain dominion before we can have a fit dwelling place. We are now gaining this dominion by mechanical means. This will be followed by the development of a human organism that, unified with Spirit, will transport us everywhere in air and on earth.

The great and most important issue before the people today is the development of man's spiritual mind and through it unity with God. There seem to be things in more immediate need of being done to alleviate present conditions, but the taproot of all this confusion is our failure to use our minds intelligently. We can only think as God would have us think by adjusting our thoughts to divine ideas. Religion and all that it implies in prayer and recognition of God in idea and manifestation is the one and only way out of the chaos in which we find ourselves. We must therefore begin at once to develop this unity with the Father mind by incorporating divine ideas into all that we think and speak.

# Chapter 9

## Demonstrating Christ Thought by Thought

*Behold, what God hath wrought!*
*An ideal man, a mighty man—*
*A man supreme, who thought by thought*
*Must demonstrate what God hath wrought.*
—CHARLES FILLMORE

Manifest man, personal man, began evolving the ideal man, that is, "putting on Christ," ages and aeons ago. We are now nearly midway in this evolution. The age of this evolution might be determined if we could count the trillions of cells in our body where are inscribed the experiences we had in the ages we have lived. However we know by inspiration and analogy that our conscious creation began with this earth. If science says the earth has been two billion years in evolving, that is our age. When the morning stars were forming we were here.

He who reads the "signs of the times" discerns spiritually that we are now in the midst of a race transition in which we are taking a very pronounced upward swing in the development of the ideal man implanted in us in the beginning. A new concept of God, man, and the universe is upon us. We must realize all this and go upward with the mighty urge for higher things. Will God take us up to an imaginary heaven in a chariot of fire, or do we use our mind to lift ourselves heavenward? "God helps those who help themselves" holds good in the heavens as in the earth. We begin right where we are to bring forth the kingdom of God within us. Every problem of life can be successfully solved if we begin with the use of the I AM on the various planes of mind. It is not we alone; it is when we realize that we can connect ourselves with the Father-Mind and prove what Jesus said—"I speak not from myself: but the Father abiding in me doeth his works"—that our potential almightiness begins to appear.

If you are given to worry and anxiety, think about the fearless confidence and trust of the Spirit. This will at once relieve your mind of the thoughts that have stirred you, and the power of the Spirit will begin its work of straightening out your affairs. If you are overwhelmed with material work and the call of the outer world, stop and concentrate in the I AM and say: "I am Spirit. I do not believe in matter or material conditions. I have power, because I know that all power is in Divine Mind. Divine Mind now sets my thoughts and all my affairs in divine order, and I rest in the confidence and peace of the kingdom within."

You can have a well body, but you must begin to build it with your word. Instead of laying up weak and sick words in your body, begin now to speak words of strength and health—and keep at it. Do not look at what has been. Lot's wife tried that, and she never got beyond the past. Clear out of your mind all rubbish about disease, and you will find that none has any lodgment in your body. The thought makes the body and determines the condition it lives in. Thoughts of health are living, eternal things, and they work with the irresistible power of almightiness to tone up the organism to their own high state of harmony and capability.

There is but one way to establish harmony in the home, and that is to establish it first in the individual. It is the law of Spirit that we must be that which we would draw to us. If we would draw to us love, we must be love, be loving and kind; if we would have peace and harmony in our environment, we must establish it within ourselves. We must faithfully and persistently deny the appearance of that which seems to be inharmonious and silently and faithfully affirm the omnipresent peace, love, and harmony that we want to see manifested. That which we hold in consciousness will be made manifest for us, therefore we should not hold the thought of anything that we do not want to see appear.

There is a relation between thinking and eating, and as you grow spiritually the character of your food and all that pertains to eating may have to be changed in conformity with the new order of things. If you will leave meat and all animal products out of your food you will see a change for the better. But above all, keep your thought mastery and do not be controlled by appetite. Do not fear to eat. Eat with thanksgiving and bless your food.

If you are looking to mental science alone for help you are certain to be disappointed; "for neither is there any other name under heaven, that is given among men, wherein we must be saved" than the name of Jesus Christ. Jesus' teaching is something deeper and farther reaching than mere mental science. It is not something that works things out for us in the personal but is a power that transforms the whole man.

Here is what Judge Troward said on this subject:

*I have studied the subject (mental science) now for several years, and have a general acquaintance with the leading features of most of the systems which unfortunately occupy attention in many circles at the present time, and I have no hesitation in saying that to the best of my judgment all sorts and descriptions of so-called occult study are in direct opposition to the real life-giving Truth.*

*We hear a great deal in these days about "initiation," but believe me, the more you try to become a so-called "initiate," the further you will put yourself from living life. I speak after many years of careful study and consideration when I say that the Bible and its revelation of Christ is the one thing really worth studying, and it is a subject large enough in all conscience, embracing as it does our outward life of everyday concerns, and also the inner springs of our life and all that we can in general terms conceive of as life.*

Just in proportion as a person yields willingly and obediently to the transforming process does he demonstrate the Truth. All that pertains to self must be put away as fast as it is revealed, and that which is of the universal, the Christ, must take its place.

Be still and witness the salvation of the Lord. You doubtless fully know that this stillness in the secret place of the Most High is not mental torpor, but a quiet tranquillity that holds itself in an equipoise of spiritual security. You have done your part when your true word has gone forth. Now rest at the center and say: "It is well; Thy work is sure; I am satisfied." Do not argue with anyone, nor discuss the matters that you have submitted to Spirit; simply say, "All is well; it is finished."

Every man who accomplishes things sees first in his mind what he wishes to do. He puts away all doubt. It makes no difference how small or how large the thing you want to do may be; if you have an unlimited confidence in your ability to do it, you will do it. Nothing can in any way impede or defeat you. Faith is the highest expression of belief or confidence. It is that something in man which says: "I believe in the possibilities of things that I cannot see. I believe in the possibility of Divine Mind doing in this age, right now, everything that was ever done in any age." When we believe this and hold to it, putting aside all doubt and whatever suggests failure, the thoughts of faith begin to accumulate substance, and fulfillment follows.

In order to realize Truth and to demonstrate it you must live it. If anyone appears careless, simply deny it and affirm order and harmony. Allow nothing in the external to disturb your poise and dominion. That is the way of love. When you refuse to see negative things they will disappear, and you will be surprised to see how you will change. Your mind, body, and affairs are the expression of your thoughts, so if you are not happy, change your mental habits. This may not seem practical to you at first, but if you will faithfully practice the Golden Rule and send only thoughts of love to everyone, you will witness practical results. You can cultivate the habit of seeing the good, the true, the bright side of every subject, and then with your friends you can bring this side out in conversation, thus keeping yourself positive and poised, and at the same time sowing the seed of Truth in the minds of others.

The "leading of the Spirit" is not something mysterious. When you open your mind to the wisdom of God in the silence, you should claim in faith that you have received, and trust that the Spirit does guide you. "Christ Jesus . . . was made unto us wisdom"; and the more you affirm that Christ is your wisdom the more you will realize the order and harmony that result from the directing power of divine wisdom. But do not be surprised and disappointed if everything does not work out according to your old ideas. The all-seeing Mind should not be judged by the dim and short vision of the mortal. What may at first seem to you failure may prove to be a clearing away of rubbish that will open the way in mind to a larger life.

Jesus showed by His life and teachings that it is the will of God for men to be well. A clear understanding of this is necessary if one wants to demonstrate health. Where there is a belief that God wills sickness and suffering, His love and power are shut out of consciousness. Spiritual healing depends on faith, and there cannot be faith while the mind is holding thoughts directly opposed to the possibility of healing. It is therefore very necessary to dwell much on the love and power of God so that a steady, unwavering faith may be established.

The subconscious realm of mind is the realm that contains all past thoughts. First, we think consciously and this thought becomes subconscious, carrying on its work of building up or tearing down, according to its character. The subconscious mind cannot take the initiative, but depends on the conscious mind for direction. When one is quickened of Spirit, one's true thoughts are set to work and the subconscious states of error are broken up and dissolved. In one's daily silence and communion with God, thoughts from the subconsciousness come into the conscious realm of mind to be forgiven and redeemed. Flesh heredity is denied and inheritance from God affirmed, which enables man consciously to draw divine ideas from the one Mind. These ideas are established in consciousness and the whole mentality is at one with Christ, the divine-man idea.

All wisdom is implanted in us by divine intelligence, which is another name for God. In the degree that we awaken to the consciousness of our inherent wisdom, in that degree we are responsible to the Father and are required to render unto Him the fruitage of our wisdom. All of us unfold according to our understanding and realization. Whether our understanding is small or large, we must measure up to or demonstrate that which has been given us. "To whomsoever much is given, of him shall much be required."

The phrase "body of Christ" has a threefold significance. First, as regards its application to the body of Jesus, in Matthew 26:26, 27, Jesus called the bread He had blessed His body and the wine His blood. Out of this came the symbolic rite of the Lord's Supper. All symbols are useful to the extent that they point man to the realities for which they stand. When this reality is discerned the symbols are understood. Jesus dwelt continually in the consciousness of being the very substance and life of God. "He that hath seen me hath seen the Father." Through the conscious realization of His oneness with God His body became a "body of life," spiritual substance, His blood the life of God. This is the body and blood He gave as a "ransom for many"; the understanding that the Christ body comes not by the grave but through our daily realization of the omnipresence of substance and life and our union with it.

Secondly, the words "body of Christ" refer to man's spiritual body. "Until Christ be formed in you." When we appropriate words of Truth, "eat them," so to speak, we partake of the substance and life of Spirit and build the Christ body. This is partaking of the body and blood of Jesus Christ, the true sacrament that vitalizes the body by renewing the mind. Every student of Truth builds the Christ body as he constantly abides in the Christ Mind through daily meditation upon words of Truth.

Thirdly, the phrase "body of Christ" applies to the group of people who find perfect unity in Spirit, free from all the limitations and authority of creed. Such a group is free from bondage to the letter and subject only to the Spirit of truth. Jesus Christ is the head of this body, and its members are joined through a recognition of universal Spirit. This "body of Christ" is sometimes referred to as the "church of Christ." This latter term is commonly misunderstood in that many sects call themselves the "church of Christ," each believing they are the chosen of God. God is not partial and does not choose. Man exercises that privilege, and if he chooses to conform to the "law of the Spirit of life in Christ Jesus" he becomes a member of the church of Christ and is recognized by the Father. There is unity only in Spirit, and "God is Spirit." All personal opinions upon which creeds are based disappear before the spiritual understanding that the only real unity is the body of Christ, His church. All who measure up to the Christ standard, forsaking everything pertaining to the personal, limited self, bringing forth the unlimited fruits of the Spirit, are members of this body, the "body of Christ." Through this body is to come the "restoration of all things, whereof God spake by the mouth of his holy prophets that have been from of old."

# Chapter 10

## Truth Radiates Light

Although Paul did not demonstrate complete over-coming, as Jesus did, he saw in man as a mystery the truth that had been lost sight of for "ages and generations . . . which is Christ in you, the hope of glory." We are urged by both Jesus and Paul to glorify God in our bodies. The body is the fruit of the mind, therefore we must become better acquainted with the mind and with the supermind in order to glorify the body.

The fact is that the entire theme of the Bible is man and his various states of mind, represented as persons, tents, tabernacles, temples. In Exodus we read, "Let them make me a sanctuary, that I may dwell among them." It is explained that this sanctuary was to be the meeting place of the people and their God and eventually the dwelling place of Jehovah. Jehovah means the I AM, which is also the meaning of the Christ or the supermind. Where in all the universe can man meet the supermind save in his own mind and body?

We are then compelled to conclude that the Tabernacle of the Israelites and the Temple of Solomon are symbols of man's body, the real meeting place of Jehovah.

Paul says, "We are a temple of the living God; even as God said, I will dwell in them, and walk in them."

When Solomon was preparing to build the Temple he soliloquized: "But who is able to build him a house, seeing heaven and the heaven of heavens cannot contain him? who am I then, that I should build him a house, save only to burn incense before him?" The burning of incense in the house of Jehovah represents the spiritualization of the fine essences of the body through adoration and exalted thoughts. When the mind is lifted up in meditation and prayer the whole body glows with spiritual light.

This spiritual light transcends in glory all the laws of matter and intellect. Even Moses could not enter the Tabernacle when it was aglow with this transcendent light.

It is written that the Israelites did not go forward on days when the cloud remained over the Tabernacle, but when the cloud was taken up they went forward. This means that there is no soul progress for man when his body is under the shadow of a "clouded" mind, but when the cloud is removed there is an upward and forward movement of the whole consciousness (all the people).

We are warned of the effect of thoughts that are against or opposed to the commandments of Jehovah. When we murmur and complain we cloud our minds, and Divine Mind cannot reach us or help us. Then we usually loaf until something turns up that causes us to think on happier things, when we go forward again.

Instead of giving up to circumstances and outer events we should remember that we are all very close to a kingdom of mind that would make us always happy and successful if we would cultivate it and make it and its laws a vital part of our life. "The joy of Jehovah is your strength."

You ask, "How can I feel the joy of Jehovah when I am poor, or sick, or unhappy?"

Jesus said, "Come unto me, all ye that labor and are heavy laden, and I will give you rest."

Here is the first step in getting out of the mental cloud that obscures the light of Spirit. Take the promises of Jesus as literally and spiritually true. Right in the midst of the most desperate situation one can proclaim the presence and power of Christ, and that is the first mental move in dissolving the darkness. You cannot think of Jesus without a feeling of freedom and light. Jesus taught freedom from mortality and proclaimed His glory so persistently that He energized our thought atmosphere into light. This light is Spirit power, and it can be seen and felt by anyone who will call on the name Christ and expect it to raise him quickly out of depression and negative states of mind into the power and zeal of an overcomer through Christ.

The Scriptures state that when Moses came down from Mount Sinai with the Ten Commandments his face shone so brilliantly that the Children of Israel and even Aaron, his own brother, were afraid to come near him until he put a veil over his face. The original Hebrew says his face sent forth beams or horns of light.

The Vulgate says that Moses had "a horned face"; which Michelangelo took literally, in his statue of Moses representing him with a pair of horns projecting from the head. Thus we see the ludicrous effect of reading the Bible according to the letter.

Our men of science have experimented with the brain in action, and they tell us that it is true that we radiate beams when we think. The force of these beams has been measured.

Here we have further confirmation of the many statements in the Bible that have been taken as ridiculous and unbelievable or as miracles.

Persons who spend much time in prayer and meditate a great deal on spiritual things develop the same type of face that Moses is said to have had. We say of them that their faces fairly shine when they talk about God and His love. John saw Jesus on the island of Patmos, and he says, "His countenance was as the sun shineth in his strength."

I have witnessed this radiance in the faces of Truth teachers hundreds of times. I well remember one class lesson during which the teacher became so eloquent that beams of light shot forth from her head and tongues of fire flashed through the room, very like those which were witnessed when the followers of Jesus were gathered in Jerusalem.

We now know that fervent words expressed in prayer and song and eloquent proclamations of spiritual Truth release the millions of electrons in our brain cells and through them blend like chords of mental music with the Mind universal.

This tendency on our part to analyze and scientifically dissect the many supposed miracles recorded in the Bible is often regarded as sacrilegious, or at least as making commonplaces of some of the very spectacular incidents recorded in Scripture.

In every age preceding this the priesthood has labored under the delusion that the common people could not understand the real meaning of life and that they should therefore be kept in ignorance of its inner sources; also that the masses could not be trusted with sacred truths, that imparting such truths to them was like casting pearls before swine.

But now science is delving into hidden things, and it is found that they all arise in and are sustained by universal principles that are open to all men who seek to know and apply them.

So the time has arrived when all shall know the Truth, "from the least to the greatest of them." Of course there are many sides to Truth. What we mean by Truth is concerned with the great fundamental questions that have always perplexed and at the same time engaged the profoundest attention of men: What is the character of God? How does God create? What is the real character of man, and what relation does he bear to his source? What is the ultimate destiny of man and the universe?

These are some of the fundamental questions that meet us at every turn. They have been answered by both philosophers and priests in every age, yet they still remain largely unanswered in the popular estimation. Of course the priests think they have the answer, but they offer no proof save that of inspiration.

The philosophers and scientists are not satisfied with the answers of the spiritually inspired. They want facts, and they are testing the seen and the unseen for forces that respond to certain laws without variation or deviation. They claim that the theological explanation of creation by Moses and the location and description of the kingdom of heaven by Jesus are not specific enough and cannot be definitely and scientifically proved; all of which is approximately true. Popular religion does not attempt to harmonize its fundamental facts with the findings of science, and in its ignorance it fights science and thinks that science is destroying the faith of the people in things spiritual.

Anyone who will search for the science in religion and the religion in science will find that they harmonize and prove each other. The point of unity is the Spirit-mind common to both. So long as religion assumes that the Spirit that creates and sustains man and the universe can be cajoled and by prayer or some other appeal can be induced to change its laws, it cannot hope to be recognized by those who know that unchangeable law rules everywhere and in everything.

Again, so long as science ignores the principle of intelligence in the evolutionary and directive forces of man and the universe, just so long will it fail to understand religion and the power of thought in the changes that are constantly taking place in the world, visible and invisible.

# Chapter 11

## The Only Mind

I say, "An idea comes to me." Where did it come from? It must have had a source of like character with its own. Ideas are not visible to the eye, they are not heard by the ear, nor felt, nor tasted, yet we talk about them as having existence. We recognize that they live, move, and have being in the realm that we term mind.

This realm of mind is accepted by everybody as in some way connected with the things that appear, but because it is not describable in terms of length, breadth, and thickness, it is usually passed over as something too vague for consideration.

But those who take up the study of this thing called mind find that it can be analyzed and its laws and modes of operation understood.

To be ignorant of mind and its laws is to be a child playing with fire, or a man manipulating powerful chemicals without knowing their relation to one another. This is universally true; and all who are not learning about mind are in like danger, because all are dealing with the great cause from which spring forth all the conditions that appear in the lives of all men and women. Mind is the one reservoir from which we draw all that we make up into our world, and it is through the laws of mind that we form our lives. Hence nothing is as important as a knowledge of mind, its inherencies, and the mode of their expression.

The belief that mind cannot be understood is fallacious. Man is the expression of mind, dwells in mind, and can know more clearly and definitely about mind than about the things that appear in the phenomenal world.

It is only from the plane of mind that one can know Truth in an absolute sense. That which we pronounce truth from the plane of appearances is relative only. The relative truth is constantly changing, but the absolute Truth endures; and what is true today always was and always will be true.

It does not require scholastic culture to understand mind. Persons who do not even know how to read or write may be very adept in the realm of pure mind. It does not follow that he who talks most fluently about mind knows the most. He may theoretically perceive the underlying principles without realizing their working factors in his own being.

Mind is not language; mind is not formulation. These are outgrowths of mind; they are man's way of communicating to his fellow man the concepts of his mind. Thus very simple persons, from the world's standpoint, frequently know a great deal about mind and its operation that they are unable to express in language.

Women as a rule know more about pure mind on its own plane than men, because they trust that inner faculty of pure knowing called intuition more fully than men. The medically wise of the world today cannot comprehend how a quiet little person who knows nothing about physiology or medication can sit down beside their dying patients and bring them back to health without apparently doing anything. And they never will know until they delve behind a knowledge of externality and learn mind to mind the workings of Spirit.

Some persons confound the realm of knowledge about things formulated through the intellect with pure knowledge. Intellect and its plane of activity are not pure mind as the realm of matter is not Spirit.

The same essences of being enter into both, but wisdom is sadly lacking in the intellectual realm. Intellect has formulated its conclusions from the sense side of existence instead of from the spiritual side, and these two sides are divergent.

No one can know about the potentialities of mind and how they are manifested except through a study of mind itself without any reference whatever to things or their relations.

One may logically deduce a system of being from abstract intellectual reasoning, but it will lack the living fire that accompanies pure mind.

Those who study mind know the same things; and though they be dumb, they enjoy the communion that ever goes on in thought. No one should for a moment imagine that because he lacks the technical education of the world that he is therefore not fitted to study the science of mind. No matter how ignorant you may be of the world's ways or God's ways, if you will give your mind to the attention of the one Mind, you will in due season become wise. This great law of mind and Mind recognizing each other and flowing together in unbroken wisdom has been known in all ages and among all peoples. The scribes and Pharisees who knew the life and lack of scholastic advantages of Jesus, the carpenter's son, exclaimed in amazement, "How knoweth this man letters, having never learned?"

Mind is the great storehouse of good from which man draws all his supplies. If you manifest life, you are confident that it had a source. If you show forth intelligence you know that somewhere in the economy of Being there is a fount of intelligence. So you may go over the elements that go to make up your being and you will find that they draw their sustenance from an invisible and, to your limited understanding, incomprehensible source.

This source we term Mind, because it is as such that our comprehension is best related to it. Names are arbitrary, and we should not stop to note differences that are merely technical. We want to get at the substance which they represent.

So if we call this invisible source Mind it is because it is of like character with the thing within our consciousness that we call our mind. Mind is manyfold in its manifestations. It produces all that appears. Not that the character of all that appears is to be laid to the volition of Mind; no, but some of its factors enter into everything that appears. This is why it is so important to know about Mind, and how its potentialities are made manifest.

So we know that that which we term Mind is the reservoir of the universe and man and that in it is stored up all that we may desire. So it behooves us to study this great reservoir and learn its laws. We call it Mind because through our study it has disclosed to us a quality that is not apprehended by those who study it in its phenomenal aspect. The physical scientist tells us that there is a universal energy in which all motion, light, heat, color, and the like, have their origin.

We claim that what they have discovered is the power side of God and that there is another factor that they have not discovered but that is associated with the universal energy. That factor is divine wisdom. They admit that there is evidence of design in the varied and beautiful manifestation of this universal energy, but they are at a loss for a way to make the acquaintance of the designer. To know this designer and manipulator of the substance and energy of the universe is what our system of mind development teaches. It instructs you how to acquaint yourself with the qualities of Mind and through them to seize upon the substance and life of the universe and bring them into harmonious relations in your body and affairs. This is something that few learned physical scientists have attempted, and here is a field of discovery upon which few have yet launched forth. In fact but few of the materialistic school have ever caught the first ray of this light. They have, it is true, longed to know more about the wisdom of the Creator, but it does not seem to have dawned upon them that the wisdom of God is just as much present everywhere as energy and substance. By all the methods known to their science they have tested the many elements of the formed and formless earth and air and noted the methodical and orderly workings of each under certain conditions. They speak of molecular attraction, repulsion, polarity, and the like. Some have said that every atom of matter is apparently intelligent; but as these atoms do not speak their particular language, they have taken for granted that they could not hold converse with them on the plane of mind.

This is where we have set up a study that makes of every atom in the universe a living center of wisdom as well as life and substance.

We claim that on its plane of comprehension man may ask the atom or the mountain the secret that it holds and it will be revealed to him. This is the communication of mind with Mind; hence we call Mind the universal underlying cause of existence and study it from that basis.

God is Mind, and man made in the image and likeness of God is Mind, because there is but one Mind, and that the Mind of God. The person in sense consciousness thinks he has a mind of his own and that he creates thought from its own inherent substance. This is a suppositional mind that passes away when the one and only real Mind is revealed. This one and only Mind of God

that we study is the only creator. It is that which origi-
nates all that is permanent; hence it is the source of all
reality. Its creations are of a character hard for the sense
man to comprehend, because his consciousness is cast in
a mold of space and time. These are changeable and tran-
sient, while the creations of the one Mind are substantial
and lasting. But it is man's privilege to understand the
creations of the one Mind, for it is through them that he
makes his world. The creations of the one Mind are ideas.
The ideas of God are potential forces waiting to be set in
motion through proper formative vehicles. The thinking
faculty in man is such a vehicle, and it is through this
that the visible universe has existence. Man does not
"create" anything if by this term is meant the producing
of something from nothing; but he does make the formless up into form; or rather it is through his conscious co-
operation that the one Mind forms its universe. Hence
the importance of man's willing co-operation with God
in every thought, because unless he is very wise in his
thinking, he may be sending forth malformations that
will cause both himself and the universe trouble.

Thinking is a process in mind by and through which
the abstract is made concrete. It is the process of working
up into things those ideas in the one Mind which are not
things. God does not see things nor conditions as man
sees them, except through the thinking faculty in man
(represented by man in the Godhead).

The ideas of Divine Mind are whole and complete
in their capacity to unfold perpetually greater and more
beautiful forms according to the thinking capacity in

man. Man catches mental sight of an idea in Divine
Mind and proceeds to put it in terms comprehensible to
him on his plane of consciousness. All ideas have their
origin in Divine Mind, but their character as unfolded by
man depends entirely upon his acquaintance with God.
The idea of a house as formulated by man varies all the
way from a wigwam to the most magnificent castle. The
original idea of a house, as it exists in God's mind, cannot be anything less than the perfected consciousness of
man, of which his body is a symbol. This is the temple
"not made with hands," and it is the only temple accept-
able to God.

No man can acceptably serve God or do His will
until he understands the fundamental principles of
thinking and how thoughts are made manifest as forms
or states of consciousness. This is revealed by the Father
to everyone who seeks to know His law and to follow it.
When man has thus sought the Father with an eye single
to His guidance, he begins to know that certain relations
exist between him and the Father and that only through
a maintenance of those relations can he come into harmony with God and do His will.

The idea of the man separated in consciousness from
Divine Mind is that he was arbitrarily created by God,
who could have chosen or not chosen to create him, and
that not being responsible for his existence, man has a
perfect right to be rebellious and petulant if hardships
come into his life. This is a childish view of the great
plan of creation, in which man is such an important fac-

tor. It is only when man becomes meek and lowly, an obedient receptacle for the Spirit of God, that he sees the divine plan of creation and his place in it. Then he becomes a willing co-operator, because his understanding accepts the law as it is and knows that it cannot be changed by either God or man. They are so intimately linked together that the harmony of existence depends upon their mutual understanding. When this is established by man's willing obedience and acceptance of his part of the work, a new order of things is set up and a new creation inaugurated. The first step in this new order is the realization by man that he is in the world to do a specific work. As Jesus said at the age of twelve, "Knew ye not that I must be in my Father's house?" and in His last prayer are these words, "I glorified thee on the earth, having accomplished the work which thou hast given me to do."

The Father has sent each one of us out to do a certain work. Are we doing that work? Have we asked what it is? Or are we aimlessly wandering about the earth trying to find satisfaction in the fleeting things of sense?

"Ye shall know the truth, and the truth shall make you free."

This truth is that of the relation of man to God and of how creation is carried forward. The God-man relation is in one sense like that of father and child; in another sense it is like that of creator-creative instrument and creation manifest. Man constitutes the instrument of God through which He brings his potentialities into visibility. As such an instrument man is in a measure a dictator as to how it shall be done. That is, man has discretionary power or free will. Freedom of will is illusionary however because if man wills to carry on creation in defiance of the divine plan and order, his creations in due time fall into chaos through lack of coherency. God fixes the plan of the structure and gives into the hands of man all the materials for building. Man may also know the plan and build according to it, or he may go ahead without consulting the plan.

Humanity has built age after age only to find that its structures do not endure. They are faulty because the divine plan has not been consulted by the builder.

Mind is the storehouse of ideas. Man draws all his ideas from this omnipresent storehouse. The ideas of God, heaven, hell, devils, angels, and all things have their clue in Mind. But their form in the consciousness depends entirely upon the plane from which man draws his mental images. If he gets a "clue" to the character of God and then proceeds to clothe this clue idea with images from without, he makes God a mortal. If he looks within for the clothing of his clue idea he knows God to be the omnipresent Spirit of existence.

If man gets the clue idea from heaven and hell and devils and angels and looks without for clothing for his idea, he makes a locality in the skies and calls it heaven, and another under the earth and calls it hell. But if he goes to the Father for information he finds both heaven and hell within his own consciousness, both the result of his own thought.

So it is of the utmost importance that we know how we have produced this state of existence which we call life; and we should be swift to conform to the only method calculated to bring harmony and success into our life, namely to think in harmony with the understanding derived from communion with the God-Mind.

# Chapter 12

## Contact with the Christ Mind

We may take it for granted on the basis of many Scripture passages that all of us who accept God as an associate in life are consciously in intimate contact with the Holy Spirit. However it will strengthen our faith and greatly add to the effectiveness of the Holy Spirit in its work with us if we understand its character and the law under which it co-operates with us in the development of mind, body, and affairs.

Theologians differ in their conceptions of the Holy Spirit. Some define it as a principle, but the majority refer to it as "He"; that is, as the third person of the Trinity. In the Scriptures it is named variously. In Genesis 1:2 it is spoken of as "the Spirit of God" moving upon the face of the waters. We read in Job 33:4:

> *"The Spirit of God hath made me,*
> *And the breath of the Almighty giveth me life."*

Bible authorities (Scofield, for example) say that wherever the name El Shaddai occurs in the Hebrew Scriptures it should have been translated "Nourisher" or "Strength-giver," which in Hebrew is the feminine name for God. This verse may be read:

*"The Spirit of God hath made me,*
*And the breath of the mother giveth me life."*

In Psalms 104:30 it is written, "Thou sendest forth thy Spirit." The Spirit is omnipresent, as revealed in the 139th Psalm:

*"Whither shall I go from thy Spirit?*
*Or whither shall I flee from thy presence?"*

Read all this psalm for a comprehension of the universality of the Holy Spirit's work in the creation of man and his evolution.

The Holy Spirit in Divine Mind corresponds to our thought in our minds. God is Mind; God's idea of His creation is His Son, and this Son (idea), executing the plans of God (the original Mind) corresponds to our thinking in its work of devising plans. We may ideate without restriction, but when we come to the execution of our ideas we have to respect certain laws, which we sometimes consider restrictions. So we can ideate the unlimited Divine Mind, but when this Mind is brought into our world or consciousness it is limited to our conception of it.

With a clear understanding of the relation that ideas bear to their manifestation, we can approach God with confidence; then we have access to the real, unlimited creative ideas, and we co-operate with the Holy Spirit and get greater results. We can thus lay hold of a healing or a prosperity thought and confidently affirm that in mind we are quickened and made whole; that we are prospered, and that we are successful in all our ways, because we are working with and through the whole Spirit of God, the Holy Spirit of wisdom and love.

In Matthew Jesus asked the Pharisees, "What think ye of the Christ? whose son is he? They say unto him, The son of David. He saith unto them, How then doth David in the Spirit call him Lord, saying,

> *"The Lord said unto my Lord,*
> *Sit thou on my right hand,*
> *Till I put thine enemies underneath thy feet?*
> *"If David then calleth him Lord, how is he his son?"*

This lesson, which Jesus gave to His disciples, brings out clearly the relation that the universal or Jehovah-Mind bears to the personal or Christ Mind. This also suggests that David was not the forebear of Christ, but that the Lord or Christ of David existed before the human person was born. It follows that the Christ in Jesus existed before the personality. This is true of all of us. Christ is the spiritual mind in every individual, and the spiritual mind is the offspring of the universal or Jehovah-Mind.

When Paul said, "Until Christ be formed in you," he referred to the development in man of the super-mind.

All the divine perfection that exists in the universal Jehovah-Mind can be brought into direct contact with its image and likeness, the Christ, imprinted in the beginning in each individual. As he develops spiritually man releases, rounds out, and fully expresses that divine perfection which is potentially in his soul.

The affirmation of any good statement of health puts us in conscious contact with the Christ Mind universal and quickens and releases the energy stored up in the subconscious mind, and the process of rejuvenation begins its work. This renewal of man's youth through the recognition of Jehovah confirms Psalm 103:

> *Bless Jehovah, O my soul;*
> *And all that is within me, bless his holy name.*
> *Bless Jehovah, O my soul,*
> *And forget not all his benefits:*
> *Who forgiveth all thine iniquities;*
> *Who healeth all thy diseases;*
> *Who redeemeth thy life from destruction;*
> *Who crowneth thee with lovingkindness and tender mercies;*
> *Who satisfieth thy desire with good things,*
> *So that thy youth is renewed like the eagle.*

All those who in faith have persistently applied this law of spiritual acknowledgment of the Christ have received benefits that bear witness to the fact that man can overcome sin, sickness, and old age and rise out of the race belief in human limitation, and finally attain eternal life as Jesus attained it.

Jesus warned us not to lay up treasure in a material way but to be "rich toward God," as taught in the 12th chapter of Luke. Jesus was rich toward God in that He knew how to release the creative substance implanted in Him from the beginning.

This same substance is within every one of us; when released, it makes contact with the universal substance, and invisible currents of supply begin to carry their riches to us. It is not necessary that we understand scientifically all the activities of the pent-up substance in our minds, although we shall eventually understand every step of the way.

A simple word of blessing poured out upon that which we have or that which we can conceive as possible for us as sons of the all-providing God will at least begin to release the superabundance of Spirit substance, and we shall have an inner confidence and faith in the providence of our Father.

Jesus warned us not to be anxious about temporal needs but to pray, believing, and to bless and give thanks; then right in the face of seeming insufficiency we should be enabled to demonstrate plenty. Jesus illustrated this when He showed how giving thanks in a devout consciousness for this inner substance would multiply the apparently insignificant resources (the five loaves and two fishes) until they became sufficient to meet the hunger of more than five thousand persons.

A textbook on the redemption or reconstruction of man should cover every phase of human character. Human egotism should be repressed; man's spiritual identity exalted. Remedies for the greatest evils of humanity should be given plentifully, and the lesser evils minimized.

Our Scriptures, plus the guidance of "the Spirit of truth" recommended by Jesus, form such a textbook for Christians. In this combination is found instruction fitted to the needs of the multitude. The timid and fearful read, "Have not I commanded thee? Be strong and of good courage; be not affrighted, neither be thou dismayed: for Jehovah thy God is with thee whithersoever thou goest."

How an inflated personal ego usurps and finally destroys the spirituality of one who once was anointed king of Israel is illustrated in the life of Saul. The stimulation of the spiritual ego is forcefully taught and demonstrated by prophets and great religious leaders. It is written in the Psalms:

*"I said, Ye are gods,*
*And all of you are sons of the Most High."*

Jesus reiterated this and was denounced by the Pharisees because He declared, "I and the Father are one."

Christian metaphysicians have discovered that man can greatly accelerate the growth in himself of the Christ Mind by using affirmations that identify him with the Christ. These affirmations often are so far beyond the present attainment of the novice as to seem ridiculous, but when it is understood that the statements are grouped about an ideal to be attained, they seem fair and reasonable.

The spiritual man is clothed by the aspirations, the thoughts, and the acts of the natural or physical man. It is here, in this realm of so-called matter, that character is formed. By faith, prayer, meditation, and inward resolutions man identifies himself with the spiritual man and forms in both mind and body the things affirmed. There was no visible evidence of Jesus' unity with the Father when He affirmed, "I and the Father are one." His disciples said, "Lord, show us the Father, and it sufficeth us." So we find that we must be true to our ideas, and clothe them with an assumption of their tangibility even before they have appeared. We must pray, believing that we have received and we shall receive.

States of mind established in the consciousness gather to themselves vitamins, cells, nerves, muscles, the flesh itself. To see oneself in mind spiritually courageous, strong, and healthy will instill health in the primal elements of the organism, which in due season will work to the surface in a perfect body.

We must all learn to look to the mental man for causes. For example, no one but a metaphysician knows the origin of disease germs. The physician takes it for granted that disease germs exist as an integral part of the natural world; the metaphysician sees disease germs as the manifested results of anger, revenge, jealousy, fear, impurity, and many other mind activities. A change of mind will change the character of a germ. Love, courage, peace, strength, and good will form good character and build bodily structures of a nature like these qualities of mind.

The same general law is carried out in everything with which man has to do. Financial success or failure depends on the attitude of mind active in both those who achieve success and those who fall under the negations of failure. To attain prosperity, think about prosperity, industry, and efficiency. Fill your mind to overflowing with thoughts of success; realize that the fullness of all good belongs to you by divine right. To this add a feeling of happiness and joy and you have the recipe for abundant and lasting prosperity.

# Chapter 13

## Metaphysics of Shakespeare

I n discussions of Shakespeare and his plays we hear little about what may be termed the by-products of the great dramatist's mind; for usually the dramatic incidents of the plays occupy the attention of the reader to the exclusion of the more subtle threads of philosophy and soul culture. Shakespeare was a great teacher, and his mind grasped the salient issues in the practical world in which he lived and often forged away ahead into realms that modern research and discovery pronounce miraculous.

Psychological insight is essential in discerning the spiritual wisdom of Shakespeare. The intellectual reader will miss entirely the references to a supermind that crop out in all his dramas. Bible readers know that spiritual things are spiritually discerned. This is also strikingly true of Shakespeare's works.

In the fantasy "Midsummer Night's Dream" Shakespeare tells how the imagination gives to airy nothings a local habitation and a name:

*I never may believe*
*These antique fables, nor these fairy toys.*
*Lovers and madmen have such seething brains,*
*Such shaping fantasies, that apprehend*
*More than cool reason ever comprehends.*
*The lunatic, the lover, and the poet*
*Are of imagination all compact:*
*One sees more devils than vast hell can hold,*
*That is, the madman: the lover, all as frantic,*
*Sees Helen's beauty in a brow of Egypt:*
*The poet's eye, in fine frenzy rolling,*
*Doth glance from heaven to earth, from earth to heaven;*
*And as imagination bodies forth*
*The forms of things unknown, the poet's pen*
*Turns them to shapes, and gives to airy nothing*
*A local habitation and a name.*
*Such tricks hath strong imagination,*
*That, if it would but apprehend some joy,*
*It comprehends some bringer of that joy;*
*Or in the night, imagining some fear,*
*How easy is a bush supposed a bear!*

In his infancy Shakespeare was baptized in the church, but his little-known history does not testify to his devotion. However his writings betray a very deep spiritual understanding. Neither was he a mystic. The fine understanding of psychology displayed by many of the Shakespearean characters must have been gained by soul development attained by the author in previous incarnations.

We should look for the antecedents of Shakespeare among the early church fathers, where the spiritual man was quickened and the culture of the soul given supreme attention. There is no record that he was taught in any schools except those of the village of Stratford, where he was born. Because of this many have asked, "Where has this man gained wisdom?"

The intellectuals have carried this lack of academic background and evidence of great supermind ability so far that they have assumed that some other person, notably Lord Bacon, is the author of Shakespeare's plays. The claim rests on very flimsy proofs and is not at all accepted by those who discern the capacity of the soul to attain understanding and carry it forward from one incarnation to another.

The claim that Shakespeare was not a scholar must be admitted. He made numerous errors of which a scholar would not be guilty. But Shakespeare was a genius of the people, not a pedant. He forged his way beyond the boundaries of the cultured intellect into the realms of fantasy and mysticism, and gave "local habitation and a name" to "airy nothing." Let us be thankful that Shakespeare was not a scholar.

Shakespeare portrayed every form of human character hundreds of years before there was such a thing as psychoanalysis, and psychologists today find in him and the puppets of his brain their most prolific examples of the subtleties of the mind.

Shakespeare did not write about himself, and we have no worldly knowledge of how such an apparently unlettered man could gain such command of language and such familiarity with men and nature. Like Jesus, he knew what was in man. Such discernment comes only with ages of experience, and we are safe in asserting that Shakespeare was a very old soul and that he inherited from previous lives a culture that made him a mastermind. We all have an untapped mind of knowledge in our subconscious mind, and it requires a mastermind to uncover it. Inspiration and rediscovery are the positive and negative poles of the mind. Shakespeare's writings indicate that he drew upon both these sources and concentrated the product in thought of the highest nobility coupled in the same scenes with shocking vulgarity. Shakespeare wrote down both what he got from the memories below and from the heavens above. Many persons whose normal thoughts are pure as snow are often shocked and puzzled at their incongruous and sometimes lascivious dreams. A maturer development will reveal that the I AM has taken advantage of the sleeping conscious mind and renewed associations with things sealed up in the depths of the subconscious mind.

That Shakespeare was familiar with a world beyond the grasp of the sense is quite evident from the words he puts into the mouths of his players. His statements about dreams, visions, witches, and prophecies, and various other references to the unseen world show that he had faith and sight above the ordinary dweller in sense.

In the play "Julius Caesar" Calpurnia, wife of Caesar, has a dream warning her of the impending danger to her husband, and she begs him not to go to the senate on the fateful day. His friends urge him to go, and he explains his reason for wanting to stay at home.

*Calpurnia here, my wife, stays me at home:*
*She dreampt to-night she saw my statue,*
*Which like a foundation with an hundred spouts,*
*Did run pure blood, and many lusty Romans*
*Came smiling and did bathe their hands in it:*
*And these does she apply for warnings and portents*
*And evils imminent, and on her knee*
*Hath begged that I will stay at home to-day.*

Decius argues that the dream has been misinterpreted. He says:

*It was a vision fair and fortunate:*
*Your statue spouting blood in many pipes,*
*In which so many smiling Romans bathed,*
*Signifies that from you great Rome shall suck*
*Reviving blood, and that great men shall press*
*For tinctures, stains, relics, and cognizance.*

Here Shakespeare reveals an acquaintance with both the literal and the allegorical meaning of dreams. Modern metaphysicians have discovered by experience that the interpretation of dreams requires the finest kind of discrimination. Some dreams are cast in the phenomenal and are given for enlightenment of the dreamer about outer events, while others are parables. Calpurnia has the discerning mind, and in the same context remarks,

*There is one within*
*Besides the things that we have heard and seen.*

The developing soul meets many situations in mind that require superior wisdom to handle. Helps of a limited character may be had from without, but the final and only safe guide is the Spirit within. The breadth and depth of Shakespeare's mind proves that he had in many lives cultivated the habit of drawing upon the fount of all wisdom within his own soul.

Spiritualists claim that spirit guidance was discovered by the Fox sisters in Hydesville, New York, less than a century ago, yet we find it portrayed in a dozen of Shakespeare's plays. Hamlet is infuriated by the graphic description by his father's ghost of his murder by the king, Hamlet's uncle. He prefaces the gruesome details with the often quoted prelude:

*I could a tale unfold whose lightest word*
*Would harrow up thy soul, freeze thy young blood,*
*Make thy two eyes, like stars, start from their spheres,*
*Thy knotted and combined locks to part*
*And each particular hair to stand on end,*
*Like quills upon the fretful porpentine.*

That Shakespeare has a certain knowledge of the status of those who have left the body is evidenced by the regrets of the ghost of Hamlet's father at his untimely violent demise.

*Of life, of crown, of queen, at once dispatched:*
*Cut off even in the blossoms of my sin,*
*Unhousel'd, disappointed, unaneled;*
*No reckoning made, but sent to my account*
*With all my imperfections on my head.*

That departed ones continue to live in a realm very near to that in which we live Shakespeare accepted as a matter of course. He makes them a vital part of so many scenes that we cannot help concluding that their existence to him was not open to question. The only place where there is any doubt suggested is in Act III, Scene 3, of "The Winter's Tale," in which Antigonus says:

*I have heard, but not believed, the spirits o' the dead*
*May walk again: if such thing be, thy mother*
*Appeared to me last night, for ne'er was dream*
*So like a waking.*

Then follows a vivid description of the mother, who "in pure white robes . . . thrice bowed before me."

Although spiritualism is not accepted by metaphysical Christians in the terms in which it is presented by its exclusive followers, it is a question of psychology and must be explained by those who teach Truth. Shakespeare did not teach religion but the facts of life as he saw them. The continuous existence of man after death of the body is one of the facts of man's spiritual life and should be so recognized and its place defined in psychology. Religion is concerned primarily with spiritual things, the psychical world is secondary.

Although he may not have applied the law of spiritual healing to himself he saw the possibility, and in many forceful phrases and subtle inferences he exalted the inherent power of man. Although Macbeth was cast in the role of a man of desperate and unsatisfied ambition, Shakespeare put into his mouth a proclamation any man can make and be strengthened by:

*The mind I sway by and the heart I bear*
*Shall never sag with doubt nor shake with fear.*

Shakespeare saw what was coming in true healing; that is, the restoration of the mind through right thinking. On this point he says:

*Canst thou not minister to a mind diseased,*
*Pluck from the memory a rooted sorrow,*
*Raze out the written troubles of the brain,*
*And with some sweet oblivious antidote*
*Cleanse the stuff'd bosom of that perilous stuff*
*Which weighs upon the heart?*

Shakespeare was familiar with all the superstitions of his age. His characters are witches, seers, soothsayers, astrologers; he shows familiarity with forces that in our day are considered occult and spooky. They believed in signs and omens, the control of men by the sun, moon, and stars—astrology. Yet the fallacy of such concepts of mortality was usually pointed out. In "King Lear" Edmund is made to say:

*This is the excellent foppery of the world, that when we are sick in fortune—often the surfeit of our own behavior—we make guilty of our disasters the sun, the moon and the stars: as if we were villains by necessity, fools by heavenly compulsion; knaves, thieves, and treachers, by spherical predominance; drunkards, liars and adulterers, by an enforc'd obedience of planetary influence; and all that we are evil in, by a divine thrusting on: an admirable evasion of whoremaster man, to lay his goatish disposition to the change of a star.*

In "Julius Caesar," where Brutus and Cassius are discussing the dominance of Caesar, Cassius says:

*Ye gods! it doth amaze me*
*A man of such feeble temper should*
*So get the start of the majestic world*
*And bear the palm alone. . . .*
*Why, man, he doth bestride the narrow world*
*Like a Colossus, and we petty men*
*Walk under his huge legs and peep about*
*To find ourselves dishonorable graves.*
*Men at some time are masters of their fates:*
*The fault, dear Brutus, is not in our stars,*
*But in ourselves, that we are underlings.*

The oft-discussed metaphysical question of the origin of evil and the source of good is settled in a concise statement by Hamlet:

"There is nothing either good or bad, but thinking makes it so."

Many years ago the London Times announced a contest to test the value that the English people placed on Shakespeare. The subject voted on was, in substance, What do you consider of the greatest value to Great Britain, Shakespeare or the Empire of India? Shakespeare won!

People the world over will readily concur in this estimate of the mind supreme in Shakespeare.

He was "not for a season, but for all time." He excelled as a dramatist, but as we have shown by these few extracts, he was also a metaphysician, a prophet, and a poet. The plots of his many plays are largely adaptations from other authors, but their glorification by Shakespeare's genius transformed them and may be likened to the glorification of the natural man by the genius of Jesus. For example, Pythagoras taught that the universe was harmonized in a masterful symphony, with suns, stars, and planets as notes on the staff supreme. Shakespeare evidently got from this his cue for the exquisite lines uttered by Lorenzo:

> How sweet the moonlight sleeps upon this bank!
> Here we will sit, and let the sounds of music
> Creep in our ears: soft stillness and the night
> Become the touches of sweet harmony.

*Sit, Jessica. Look how the floor of heaven*
*Is thick inlaid with patines of bright gold:*
*There's not the smallest orb which thou behold'st*
*But in his motion like an angel sings,*
*Still quiring to the young-eyed cherubins;*
*Such harmony is in immortal souls;*
*But whilst this muddy vesture of decay*
*Doth grossly close it in, we cannot hear it.*

# Chapter 14

## The Body

A great deal is said in the Bible about man's body. In fact, the Bible is a mystical record of the various bodies in which the souls of men have lived. Bodies show the different states of mind of those who inhabit them, ranging all the way from the Adam embodiment and environment up to the Christ body and its freedom from environment. It is fair to say that the Bible is the allegorical record of man under many aliases, in many bodies.

In all the history of man he has appeared under all sorts of masks, which he has called his bodies, ranging from a corrupt and distorted body up to the "glorious body" of Christ.

The resurrection of the body is the paramount theme of the New Testament and in fact the all-embracing yet veiled subject of the entire Bible. Immortality has been the engrossing subject of man's thought since the record of the race began. Passage after passage might be cited from the Bible illustrating what man's body potentially is and how it should be controlled and governed so as to gain for its possessor the greatest amount of harmony in life.

Now, mark you, man is not solely his body, for man is more than body, but without a body there could be no visible man. Yet the body is not man, but man will forever possess a body. If the body is not man and man could not be without a body, and since the body is constantly changing, what is man?

You see at once that man is not body, but that the body is the declaration of man, the substantial expression of his mind. We see so many different types of men that we are bound to admit that the body is merely the individual's specific interpretation of himself, whatever it may be. Man is an unknown quantity; we see merely the various ideas of man expressed in terms of body, but not man himself. The identification of man is determined by the individual himself, and he expresses his conception of man in his body.

Some persons have tall bodies; some have short ones. Some have fat bodies; some have slim ones. Some have distorted bodies, some have symmetrical ones. Now, if the body is the man, as claimed by sense consciousness, which of these many bodies is man?

The Bible declares that man is made in the "image" and after the "likeness" of God. Which of the various bodies just enumerated is the image and likeness of God?

The New Testament maintains that man's body is the dwelling place of the Spirit of God: "Know ye not that your body is a temple of the Holy Spirit which is in you? . . . glorify God therefore in your body." Yet it is written that the Man of Galilee casts devils out of this temple of God. How could devils infest the temple of God?

Some persons contend that man's body is corrupt from birth, and others affirm that it is the glorious masterpiece of God.

We find however that those who say that they despise the body are loath to part with it, for the reason that they cannot adequately conceive of man without a body, and it is better to have some kind of a body than to run the risk of not having any. The body that these persons possess is their only means of identifying themselves. They do not fancy the idea of risking another, and possibly a worse body, so they hold onto the one they have as long as they are able, regardless of its frailties. The chances of getting a new body seem so uncertain that we all strive to keep the one we have.

Let us repeat that the body of man is the visible record of his thoughts. It is the individual's interpretation of his identity, and each individual shows in his body just what his views of man are. The body is the corporeal record of the mind of its owner, and there is no limit to its infinite differentiation. The individual may become any type of being that he elects to be. Man selects the mental model and the body images it. So the body is the image and likeness of the individual's idea of man. We may embody any conception of life or being that we can conceive. The body is the exact reproduction of the thoughts of its occupant. As a man thinks in his mind so is his body.

You can be an Adam if you choose, or you can be a Christ or any other type of being that you see fit to ideate. The choice lies with you. The body merely executes the mandates of the mind. The mind dictates the model according to which the body shall be manifested. Therefore as man "thinketh within himself [in his vital nature], so is he." Each individual is just what he believes he is.

It is safe to say that nine hundred and ninety-nine persons out of every thousand believe that the resurrection of the body has something specifically to do with the getting of a new body after death; so we find more than ninety-nine per cent of the world's population waiting for death to get something new in the way of a body. This belief is not based on the principles of Truth, for there is no ready-made-body factory in the universe, and thus none will get the body that he expects. Waiting for death in order to get a new body is the folly of ignorance. The thing to do is to improve the bodies that we now have; it can be done, and those who would follow Jesus in the regeneration must do it.

The "resurrection" of the body has nothing whatever to do with death, except that we may resurrect ourselves from every dead condition into which sense ignorance has plunged us. To be resurrected means to get out of the place that you are in and to get into another place. Resurrection is a rising into new vigor, new prosperity; a restoration to some higher state. It is absurd to suppose that it applies only to the resuscitation of a dead body.

Paul hints at a time when the body will be changed, and he says it is when "death is swallowed up in victory." Here are Paul's words: "When this corruptible shall have put on incorruption, and this mortal shall have put on immortality . . . Death is swallowed up in victory."

This transformation is worked out by the individual himself, and is not the result of physical death but rather of the death or annihilation of the erroneous beliefs that ignorance has stored in the cells of the body. It is first a mental resurrection, followed by a body demonstration.

It is the privilege of the individual to express any type of body that he sees fit to ideate. Man may become a Christ in mind and in body by incorporating into his every thought the ideas given to the world by Jesus.

"But we all, with unveiled face beholding as in a mirror the glory of the Lord, are transformed into the same image from glory to glory, even as from the Lord the Spirit."

Divine mind has placed in the mind of everyone an image of the perfect-man body. The imaging process in the mind may well be illustrated by the picture that is made by light on the photographic plate, which must be "developed" before it becomes visible. Or man's invisible body may be compared to the blueprint of a building that the architect delivers to the builder. Man is a builder of flesh and blood. Jesus was a carpenter. Also He was indeed the master mason. He restored the Lord's body ("the temple of Jehovah") in His mind and heart (in Jerusalem).

When we call ourselves fleshly, mortal, finite, we manifest it bodily upon a fleshly, mortal, and finite plane. We sow to the flesh and of the flesh reap corruption. The time has arrived for the whole human family to repudiate the estimate of man as corrupt and instead to think of him as he was designed by creative Mind. "This corruptible must put on incorruption, and this mortal must put on immortality," said Paul.

We must stop calling the body flesh and blood, and see it as it is in Spirit-mind, pure and incorruptible. This realization of man's perfect body will arrest decay, disintegration, and death.

We must rise above material thoughts into spiritual realization, and live, move, and have our being in a divine reality. When our views of man are elevated to spiritual understanding, we shall begin to express bodily perfection. Our thoughts must be perfect before we can expect to manifest perfection in body. The issues of life are within man; the body is merely the record of the mind of the individual.

Jesus demonstrated for us the highest type of embodiment. He brought His body under the mastery of His mind. He said, "I have power to lay it down, and I have power to take it again." What Jesus did we all can do, and it is fair to say that His is the normal standard for every individual and that every other expression of life is abnormal, the result of insufficient Christ elements. Paul says, as quoted, "Ye are the body of Christ," and he says this to emphasize the fact that Christ is the one true pattern for man and that each of us should achieve the fulfillment of the divine design. "Let us make man in our image, after our likeness."

Jesus was the only man who ever proclaimed with authority, "He that hath seen me hath seen the Father." Jesus was the divine oracle; His mind was unified with the universal Mind principle; this same principle obtains in a degree today in those who identify themselves with Spirit instead of with the flesh. We need not "look . . . for another" in whom to witness the Christ, as did John the Baptist, but we must look for Christ in ourselves, precisely as the man Jesus found the Christ in Himself.

The statement "Ye are the body of Christ" promises the possibility of a universal incarnation of the Christ and does not in any sense narrow it down to one single individual.

Again Paul's words "Glorify God . . . in your body" proclaim the fact that the God nature may become manifest in every individual. What is the chief object of man? To glorify God in his body; this is the true answer. Have the courage to make the heroic attempt to give personal expression to God. And how shall we do this? By mentally agreeing that we are potentially the Christ and capable of making a divine presentation of ourselves to the Father. We must rise to the conscious realization that every thought of mind, every atom of body, every molecule of being, every function of nature, and every force is divine, and that all of these do and shall vibrate to the harmonies of Spirit. This is the resurrection of man; there is none other.

By so doing we establish our ego, our I AM identity with Divine Mind, and enter with Jesus into joint heirship to the heavenly inheritance of power, peace, prosperity, and perfection.

All the so-called human or earthly spheres of operation are reflections of the divine, and by considering them we may gain an intellectual concept of spiritual realities, but we should ever remember that spiritual things are "spiritually judged." By this higher renewal of the mind we shall be bodily transformed, and prove those things that are good, perfect, and true.

The resurrection of the body is not dependent for its demonstration on time, evolution, or any of the man-made means of growth. It is the result of the elevation of the spiritually emancipated mind of the individual.

Step by step, thought added to thought, spiritual emotion added to spiritual emotion—eventually the transformation is complete. It does not come in a day, but every high impulse, every pure thought, every upward desire adds to the exaltation and gradual personification of the divine in man and to the transformation of the human. The "old man" is constantly brought into subjection, and his deeds forever put off, as the "new man" appears arrayed in the vestments of divine consciousness.

All have hope and find deep consolation, aye, assurance in the belief of the final redemption of the body; and this universal feeling is born of the legitimacy of the faith that this redemption must eventuate, that perfection is the ultimate goal of man's being, and that death and separation must disappear from human experience.

How to accomplish the resurrection of the body has been the great stumbling block of man. The resurrection has been a mere hope, and we have endeavored to reconcile a dying body with a living God, but have not succeeded. No amount of Christian submission or stoical philosophy will take away the sting of death. But over him who is risen in Christ "death no more hath dominion."

# Chapter 15

## Faith Precipitations

When asked what electricity is, a scientist replied that he had often thought of it as an adjunct to faith, judging from the way it acts.

This linking of faith and electricity seems at first glance fantastic, but when we observe what takes place when certain substances in solution and an electric current are brought in conjunction, there seems to be a confirmation of the Scripture passage: "Now faith is assurance of things hoped for."

Just as the electric current precipitates certain metals in solution in acid, so faith stirs into action the electrons of man's brain; and acting concurrently with the spiritual ethers, these electrons hasten nature and produce quickly what ordinarily requires months of seedtime and harvest.

The widow, in the time of Elisha, was so distressed with debt that she had even mortgaged to slavery her two children. She appealed to the prophet, who said, "What hast thou in the house?" She replied, "Thy handmaid hath not anything in the house, save a pot of oil." He told her to borrow all the empty vessels her neighbors had and then to go into the house and shut the door, and to pour the oil in the pot into all those vessels; which she did until they were all full. She then paid her debts and had plenty left.

Jesus fed four thousand persons at one time and five thousand at another by the same means. He also "precipitated" the elements of wholeness many times and healed the multitude. He required co-operation in faith on the part of those He healed in order thus to complete the healing circuit.

Speedy answers to prayer have always been experienced and always will be when the right relations are established between the mind of the one who prays and the spiritual realm, which is like an electrical field. The power to perform what seems to be miracles has been relegated to some God-selected one; but now we are inquiring into the law, since God is no respecter of persons, and we find that the fulfillment of the law rests with man or a group of men, when they quicken by faith the spiritual forces latent within them.

The reason why some prayers are not answered is lack of proper adjustment of the mind of the one who prays to the omnipresent creative spiritual life.

Jesus was the most successful demonstrator of prayer of whom we have any record, and He urged persistence in prayer. If at first you don't succeed, try, try again. Like Lincoln, Jesus loved to tell stories to illustrate His point, and He emphasized the value of persistence in prayer.

He told of a woman who demanded justice of a certain judge and importuned him until in sheer desperation he granted her request.

Every Christian healer has had experiences where persistent prayer saved his patient. If he had merely said one prayer, as if giving a prescription for the Lord to fill, he would have fallen far short of demonstrating the law. Elijah prayed persistently until the little cloud appeared or, as we should say, he had a "realization"; then the manifestation followed.

The Bible is treasured as the word of God because it records so many of these apparent miracles; but the fact is that all over this land enough demonstrations of the supermind are taking place every day to fill many books of the size of the Bible. Some of them are recorded, and people read about them, but these are few compared with the many that are taking place. All of which goes to prove that there is a restorative law that, if taken advantage of, will heal the world of all its ills.

Many of the old-school faith healers object to the scientific explanation of the healing process. They have believed in a personal God and that all superworld forces are set in motion by His personal intervention. However it is much more satisfying to logical minds to know that God is the law and that the Spirit that we have thought of as a projection of Him is in fact He Himself in His own spiritual identity. This is the teaching of Jesus, and our men of science are proving it to be true. An understanding of this all-accessible Truth is making seers, prophets, and mighty men of God out of pygmies. On every hand men of mediocre ability are becoming world leaders through exploiting the supermind qualities that they have merely glimpsed as existing within them.

These ephemeral Caesars have gained in inkling of the disciplined mind's dominion and are using it to control the negative mass thought, and through the hypnotic force of words they evolve chaos and dark night the world over.

When men accept and understand Jesus' teaching about the mastery of the spiritual man, all the evils that arise from these upstart saviors will disappear. But now in the night of mind's eclipse

> *"We petty men*
> *Walk under his huge legs, and peep about*
> *To find ourselves dishonorable graves."*

Then the question arises, If this supermind ability is in every man, why is it not more widely understood and used?

There are several answers to this pertinent question, the most plausible being the lack of human initiative. Men prefer to let others do their thinking for them. This is especially true in religious matters. The race thought has been so saturated with the belief that spiritual revelation must come through some authorized channel that the man without an ecclesiastical degree is timid about expressing an opinion about God or man's spiritual nature.

Jesus broke this hypnotic spell when without ecclesiastical authority He claimed to be the Son of God.

We should remember that Jesus included as sons of God all those who, as He said, are "my sheep," that is, follow Him. He quoted Psalm 82, in which it is written,

*"I said, Ye are gods,*
*And all of you sons of the Most High."*

The church elders and the people cried, "Crucify him!" Jesus taught great truths, which were grasped by but a few open-minded followers, and they formed a new church. After doing mighty works for hundreds of years they in turn, built an ecclesiastical hierarchy from which the common people were excluded. The Church Fathers gathered and selected certain religious manuscripts and compiled the Bible, which they proclaimed to be the very word of God, to be read and interpreted by those only having the authority of the church.

Here again we see positive thought submitting to negative thought, thereby keeping the world in darkness for ages.

As Luther started the Protestant Reformation so we are now at the beginning of another reformation, in which the freedom and power of man spiritually will not only be taught but demonstrated.

The supermind demonstrations that mark this modern religious reformation seem so at variance with nature that they are still looked upon as miracles, notwithstanding the fact that logic and science shout from the housetops the universality of law.

Those who study the spiritual import of Jesus' teaching have revealed to them a mental technique for which no adequate language has yet been invented.

The Jews demanded of Jesus that He tell them plainly, and His reply was that His works would testify that He was the Son of God and that He and the Father were one. We who have experienced Spirit baptism freely testify to the dynamic thrill that ripples through the nerves for days and months and is often repeated in silent meditation for years after the first outpour. Thus revelation, observation, and actual experience prove that man develops spirituality according to the divine pattern called in Genesis the image and likeness of God.

The natural man in the physical world is merely the beginning formation of the man planned by creative Mind. When the natural man finishes his unfoldment he enters the next stage, that of the Christ man illustrated by Jesus. Jesus was the first man or "fruit" of the earth's first age, that of the natural man. He opened the way for all those who aspire to the attainment of immortality.

To the present time the followers of Jesus have been told by spiritual leaders that He taught the immortality of the soul only. But now it is revealed that He immortalized His body and said, "Follow me." It was man's sins that brought death to his body, and his redemption must include the healing of the body. When the mind is healed of its sins the body will respond. "Your body is a temple of the Holy Spirit, which is in you, which ye have from God."

So we find as we study and apply the doctrine of Jesus that the body must be included. Faith in the omnipresent pure substance precipitates the substance in the body and we are transformed.

Proofs may be found in profusion that the divine law of body restoration is in action in a large way right here in our midst. The literature of Unity teems with testimonials of persons who have been healed and are grateful to God for renewed health, strength, prosperity, and happiness. Thus it is not necessary to strengthen your faith by reading about the work of God in ages past; you can personally consult your neighbor, who can doubtless tell you of marvels fully as great as any recorded in the Bible.

The majority of cases that come to us belong to the class of the discouraged woman told of in Luke 8:43, "who spent all her living upon physicians, and could not be healed." Doctors have pronounced them incurable, and as a last resort they turn to God. The hardest part of the work in their healing is to get out of their minds the verdict of the doctor that their cases are incurable. We have discovered that there are no incurables. "With God all things are possible." Any experienced metaphysical healer will tell you that he has been the instrument through which all the popular diseases have been healed.

Some of the stories told by patients are beyond human credence; for example, the restoration of the eyes of a man from which they had been removed, and the growth of the nose of a woman who had lost it by disease. These are very rare but well authenticated in metaphysical circles. I am not prepared to give the names of these cases, but I can testify to my own healing of tuberculosis of the hip. When a boy of ten I was taken with what was at first diagnosed as rheumatism but developed into a very serious case of hip disease. I was in bed over a year, and from that time an invalid in constant pain for twenty-five years, or until I began the application of the divine law. Two very large tubercular abscesses developed at the head of the hip bone, which the doctors said would finally drain away my life. But I managed to get about on crutches, with a four-inch cork-and-steel extension on the right leg. The hip bone was out of the socket and stiff. The leg shriveled and ceased to grow. The whole right side became involved; my right ear was deaf and my right eye weak. From hip to knee the flesh was a glassy adhesion with but little sensation.

When I began applying the spiritual treatment there was for a long time slight response in the leg, but I felt better, and I found that I began to hear with the right ear. Then gradually I noticed that I had more feeling in the leg. Then as the years went by the ossified joint began to get limber, and the shrunken flesh filled out until the right leg was almost equal to the other. Then I discarded the cork-and-steel extension and wore an ordinary shoe with a double heel about an inch in height. Now the leg is almost as large as the other, the muscles are restored, and although the hip bone is not yet in the socket, I am certain that it soon will be and that I shall be made per-fectly whole.

I am giving minute details of my healing because it would be considered a medical impossibility and a miracle from a religious standpoint. However I have watched the restoration year after year as I applied the power of thought, and I know it is under divine law. So I am satisfied that here is proof of a law that the mind builds the body and can restore it.

# Chapter 16

## The Seed Is the Word

Being has two aspects: the invisible and the visible, the abstract and the concrete. The visible comes forth from the invisible, and this coming forth is always according to a universal method of growth from minute generative centers. All forms are built according to this law. From center to circumference is the method of growth throughout the universe. The one who studies form alone and expects to learn from it and its transformations the secret of existence never goes back to the "seed"; never catches sight of the Spirit moving upon every generating center.

Causes are always invisible: spiritual. "God is spirit," and "the seed is the word of God." Thus that which produces the seed is the Spirit. It is popularly presumed that the seed produces after its kind that which appears. This is a superficial conclusion, and a moment's logical consideration will convince anyone that a thing so small, a cause so insignificant as compared with the effect, could not produce without being possessed of an anterior principle results so large and varied. The oft-repeated illustration of the acorn's having folded within its heart the oak is not correct. The acorn of itself is powerless to produce anything, but as an avenue through which interior forces become exterior it is important.

We should never lose sight of the fact that things are but the evidence of intelligence and power. In and of themselves they are without causative power in any way. The seed is the symbol of the Word of God, and in its generative qualities it represents the apparent insignificance of the Word as it goes forth from its invisibility and silence. But this Word is a generative center with all the possibilities of God at its call. It is the idea of God, the image and likeness. It is just like God in its essentials, and needs only to be planted in fertile ground to produce the living picture of which it is the image. In its highest degree of expression this is man. Christ is the Word of God. It was in the beginning with God, and is now with God. It came forth from God. It became flesh and dwelt among men. It always dwells among men; it is the real originating center through which man draws all his intelligence, life, love, substance. It is the one point at which we tap the divine storehouse; it is the inlet and outlet of God.

So the "seed," that is, "the word of God," is man; not the external thinking personality that has a consciousness of separation, but the internal spiritual germ. The central seed is the generative center from which the personal man forms himself. He draws upon the universal forces within and without, just as the tree draws upon the invisible Spirit, manifesting itself in earth, air, and water. He may be totally unconscious of this situation in certain stages of his building, but this does not nullify the fact. The fact that the babe is not conscious of the method of its sustenance during the first months of its prenatal life has no weight with those who have observed the law.

Man is the idea of God, and the idea of God is the word of God. Man is not a thing of small beginnings but of infinite beginnings. His resource is the Infinite, and he draws his substance from an inexhaustible store. He is never at a loss for supply, be it ever so scarce in the markets of the world.

At the heart center of everyone is the "seed . . . the word of God." It is there as a door opening into the infinite. Man opens this door or closes it at his will. Some open it just a little crack and others not at all. Some open the door wide, and they manifest such rare powers that they are exalted, even deified, by those who have closed their own doors. This little inner door is a door of great promise; he who opens it wide finds on its inner side the kingdom of God. It is the way into the kingdom. It is the Christ Spirit speaking through those who have opened: "I am the door."

It is strange but true that the inner "seed" of God may have been so neglected as to have been entirely forgotten by some people. They may have a slight recollection of having at some remote period been in a state in which they did not have to endure the burdens of self-sustenance, but this is so faint that it is like a dim, faraway dream. When a man has thus forgotten the seed and has sought other means of growth, he loses his symmetry. He becomes gnarled and crooked. His body is filled with knots, and his limbs die before their time. This is the paralysis of nonrecognition of the generative seed. No true growth results from earth and air alone. Man does not live by bread alone, but by every word proceeding out of the mouth of God. This "word of God" is the "seed"; that is, man's real self, because it is the umbilical cord that forever connects him with the infinite fountain of supply. No growth takes place except through this "seed," this high idea of what man is. Any other idea is a reflection, and there are reflections in descending degree, until man finds himself comparing himself with his own creations—worm of the dust.

As Emerson says:

*Whilst a necessity so great caused the man to exist, his health and erectness consists in the fidelity with which he transmits influences from the vast and universal to the point on which his genius can act. The ends are momentary; they are vents for the currents of inward life which increases as it is spent. A man's wisdom is to know that all ends are momentary, that the best end must be superseded by a better. But there is a mischievous tendency in him to transfer his thoughts from the life to the ends, to quit his agency and rest in his acts: the tools run away with the workman, the human with the divine. I conceive a man as always spoken to from behind, and unable to turn his head and see the speaker. In all the millions who have heard the voice, none ever saw the face. As children in their play run behind each other, and seize one by the ears and make him walk before them, so is the spirit our unseen pilot. That well-known voice speaks in all languages, governs all men, but none ever catches a glimpse of its form. If the man will exactly obey it, it will adopt him, so that he shall not any longer separate it from himself in his thought; he shall seem to be it, he shall be it. If he listen with insatiable ears, richer and greater wisdom is taught him; the sound swells to ravishing music, he is borne away as with a flood, he becomes careless of his food and of his house, he is the tool of ideas, and leads a heavenly life. But if his eye is set on the things to be done, and not on the truth that is still taught, and for the sake of which the things are to be done, then the voice grows faint, and at last is but a humming in his ears. His health and greatness consist in his being the channel through which heaven flows to earth, in short, in the fullness in which an ecstatical state takes place in him. It is pitiful to be an artist, when by forbearing to be artists we might be vessels filled with the divine overflowings, enriched by the circulations of omniscience and omnipresence.*

Let not this seed of God within you lie fallow for want of conscious recognition on your part. You want to express all the possibilities of Being, which you can do if you will acknowledge the source through which they methodically come forth.

Many people think man grows a little differently from other things. They are sure he is a special creation, formed by the Lord God in a miraculous way, from the "dust of the ground" and "set up against de palin's to dry"! This style of creation will do for the backwoods preacher but not for thinking people. Man is the creation of God. God creates in a definite manner. Man is created in a definite manner. He comes forth into the visible world in a regular, everyday sort of a way, through the simple process wrapped up in the mystery of this inner "seed."

To think that man is created in any but a methodical way is to think without reasonable consideration. There is no evidence anywhere of a miraculous creation of anything, and it is folly to assume that the Almighty stepped out of His course to make man. Man in his divine selfhood makes himself. His process is precisely that of God's, through the power of his word. Without the Christ word man has no life in him. Man does not make anything that lasts unless it has its point of departure in this inner seed idea of the Father. Men think they are building, but they are deceived. They may spend thousands of years rearing states of consciousness that in the day of judgment between the real and the evanescent must be dissolved into the vapor of nothingness.

Every idea is a seed, and will bring forth according to its character, modified somewhat by the kind of mind soil in which it is planted. There is a law of growth in mind parallel with that of earth. A thistle seed will always produce thistles, regardless of the character of the soil; a low ideal will likewise work out low conditions in a high type of mind. You may be a giant in strength today, but if you get into your mind the thought of sickness it will bring you down as surely as if you were a weakling. So with every thought that finds lodgment and at the same time credence in your mind; it will produce fruit of its kind just as surely as will the material seed planted in the earth. It goes through a similar process of growth also. It does not always spring forth at once and rapidly come to fruition, but it goes through a methodical series of changes, from inertness to tiny sprout, away deep down in the consciousness, where it is not observed by the external thinking mind. In due course it sends out a shoot in the direction of external consciousness, which finally comes to the surface in some discord or some harmony. The time of planting is usually so remote that even he who knows the law of growth from thought to thing cannot remember when he sowed the seeds that are manifest in his consciousness as thistles. When told that certain thoughts have produced certain effects in his case, the patient will invariably respond, "But I was not thinking those thoughts."

One of the first lessons to be learned by the student of metaphysics is that the "seed is the word." The next is that this kind of seed is hid in the darkness of the mind, where it germinates, sprouts, and comes into visibility with all the scientific accuracy of detail of the ordinary plant. The fruit is a living organism too and has the power to throw off seeds that find lodgment and produce crops in other receptive minds.

But each man is a gardener who has absolute charge of his mind and can determine just what kind of seeds shall be planted in his domain. What he says is law in the garden of which he has control. If he is lax, shiftless, and ignorant of his privileges, he may let the thistle seeds from foolish minds blow over his fence and take root in his garden. But it is not at all necessary. By his simple word of command he can protect his domain from all intruders. Not all men know this, nevertheless it is true.

# Chapter 17

## The Resurrecting Power of the Word

I t is plainly taught in the Bible that God created a spiritual, undying man; that death came into the world through transgression of the law, called sin; that sin was the work of one man, and that sin would be overcome by one man. "As in Adam all die, so in Christ shall all be made alive." Jesus Christ is the fulfillment of that promise.

The race has so long existed in the negative mental conditions that bring sickness and finally death that it is very difficult to convince men that they can live forever in their bodies. They have been taught that death is natural, that death is part of the scheme of life, that through death we progress to better conditions. This negative teaching has been a part of the race thought so long that death has been accepted as the necessary end of existence. But such is not the teaching of Christianity.

Every organ of the body is capable of being constantly renewed through the inflow of an unseen force called mind or life or Spirit. Therefore we should be continually renewing and spiritualizing the body. But we are not doing so because of our lack of faith in our possibilities as offspring of universal life. We find it hard to believe that the renewing and spiritualizing of the body can be accomplished, yet the history of the Hebrew race (considered as an allegory) shows that this is possible.

We look on the wanderings of the Children of Israel in the wilderness as typical of our wanderings through the wilderness of materiality and ignorance on our way to the Promised Land; but we have always put the Promised Land away off somewhere in heaven! The teaching of Jesus is that we can demonstrate over all the ills of the body, all the discords and inharmonies of the flesh, and finally overcome death as He did, here and now.

The lesson of Easter, when learned, convinces us that one man demonstrated what has been taught throughout the centuries in the religion of Christianity. Jesus evidently did not know in the beginning of His life that He was to make this great demonstration. He was a carpenter and worked with Joseph, but for thirty years He must have been growing in spiritual power. In meditation He doubtless caught glimpses of the great Truth, and it dawned on Him that He was the man who had been selected, or that through His own demonstration He had attained the ability, to overcome the negative thoughts, the sins that were tearing down the bodies of the race, and that He had the power to gain complete mastery of the human weakness called death.

When Jesus received the illumination and stepped forth as a teacher, He found it very difficult to impress on others that He was anything more than one of the common people. He claimed immortality, He claimed that He was the Messiah they had been looking for, and they said in effect: "This is ridiculous. We know this man. He is Jesus, the son of Mary and Joseph. We know Him and His brothers and His sisters. We have been brought up with Him. It is absurd to think that a man can step right out of the common herd and become the Messiah."

It is an adage that a great man is not without honor except in his own country. From the physical viewpoint we are part of the common people and we will not concede that one of our number can by any possibility become divine. The Scriptures plainly teach that Jesus' own followers did not believe His claim that He was divine. They admitted that He was a great teacher. He taught truths that they accepted in the abstract, but they were not ready to concede that one of their number had attained the demonstration of Truth. In a sort of wonderment Jesus' disciples followed Him, but they had not grasped the underlying truths that He was teaching: that the body is the temple of the living God, and that the man Jesus could lay it down or take it up; that He was going to make a demonstration over death that would satisfy not only them but the whole world; that when He was ready He was going up to Jerusalem to be crucified there. Christian metaphysicians see symbology in all this, but it actually took place.

Jesus knew that He must demonstrate over death and that He must prepare for that test. He told all His friends that He was going to accomplish this thing, but they were incredulous. Peter attempted to dissuade Jesus from His announced purpose of going to

Jerusalem to be crucified, but Jesus would not be swerved from His course. We often think that if Jesus would only come now and make a demonstration over death, we should all believe. Probably only a handful of us would accept Him if He came among us today and made such a demonstration. The newspapers would say it was a fake, a trick. The scribes and the Pharisees and the doubters reported that the soldiers were paid to open the tomb and let Jesus escape. Incredulity exists today. That is the reason why the demonstration of eternal life is so difficult. That is the reason why after two thousand years the world at large is not convinced that it is possible for man to be raised out of the thought that death is inescapable. Even after Jesus demonstrated resurrection the disciples found it hard to believe Him.

A woman was the first person to come to Jesus' tomb after His resurrection. Women are more receptive to Truth than men. Women have more spirituality and faith than men, but if today a man died who had claimed that he would resurrect his body on a certain day, it is doubtful whether even the women would go to the tomb to see that resurrection. Mary and the other women did not go to the tomb of Jesus expecting Him to be there alive. They did not expect to see Him come out of the tomb; on the contrary they had spices and herbs for the embalming of His body. The body was not there and they began to inquire about it. The angel told them, "He is risen"; but they could not believe it, and they looked into the tomb. There were the grave clothes, but the body of Jesus was gone. The disciples, when told that Jesus had risen, were skeptical. We are told that Jesus walked with two of them on the way to Emmaus and explained the Scriptures to them. After a time they recognized Him; then He disappeared from their midst.

Shortly after the incident at Emmaus Jesus appeared again to the Eleven, and to prove to them that He had the same body that He had had before His resurrection, He "showed them his hands and his feet," and He ate a piece of broiled fish. After that He disappeared again. All this would be thought "spooky" in our day, and we cannot blame the apostles for being "amazed."

Followers of Jesus do not understand the difference between the astral or ghostly body of the dead and the resurrected body of Jesus. There is a difference made by the mental power of the individual and the way he thinks about life, soul, spirit, and matter.

If we believe that the body is the temple of the living God, we shall follow Jesus in the resurrection.

Why are we not resurrecting the body? Why are we giving it up to disintegration? Sin is the cause of death; then it must be that through the elimination of sin we shall come into eternal life and save the body from the disintegrating effects of death. In fact we are all striving for the resurrection of the body when we try to overcome its oncreeping feebleness. But our efforts are material instead of spiritual. We should remember that "it is the spirit that giveth life; the flesh profiteth nothing." We try in many ways to renew the life supply within us.

Some very absurd methods have been advocated by so-called scientists to perpetuate man's life, to make him healthier, wealthier, happier. We all want more life, more happiness, more good; and we can have everything we want if we comply with the divine law as Jesus did. The body is composed of elements that are essentially perfect. We have not understood the law of harmony and have therefore thrown these primal perfect elements out of adjustment. By our thoughts we are continually moving the cells of the body. The original impetus is given by the conscious mind, hence we must regulate our thinking to the end that harmony be set up in the cellular life throughout the organism.

It is very evident that Jesus understood the science of right thinking. We hate our enemies and have bodily disorders as a result. Jesus said, "Love your enemies." This is but one of many laws of mind activity that Jesus carried out in His life. We must first follow Jesus in controlling our thoughts; then we shall be able to follow Him in the resurrection.

Jesus controlled His thoughts by harmonizing them, by continually thinking constructively, by continually bringing into action in His conscious mind all the mental factors that lead to the new life, to the understanding of what life is. We know that the body is destroyed by discord, by fever, and by other inharmonies. Fever is but a clashing of the cells of the organism, a tearing down process; but back of fever are harsh thoughts. We can trace every ill to some thought. We must eliminate these sinning thoughts. The sinning thought is the thought that fails to measure up to the high calling; it is not a true thought. We have limited our ideas to a small realm. We have thought that sin covered only the transgressions of the moral man. But I assure you that sin becomes visible in the physical; hence we should look for a physical resurrection after we have crucified the carnal mind.

Jesus laid great stress on the power of the word. The word has two activities: One is that of the still small voice in the silence, and the other is that of the "loud voice" that was used by Jesus when He raised Lazarus from the dead. In the beginning "God said, Let there be"—and there was.

We are the offspring of God, and our words have power proportionate to our realization of our in-dwelling spiritual kingdom. In the world today there is ample evidence of the power of words to move multitudes. That same power can heal and make people happy. If you will recognize this power and increase it and apply it in all your thoughts and acts, the impetus given to your spoken thought will produce a body so constructed, so harmonized that it will renew itself and never allow you to go to the grave. Jesus did a work of this kind. He said that a man would be held accountable for his slightest word. Jesus sent His word to heal people. He said, "If a man keep my word, he shall never taste of death." What were His words? They were words of life, of peace, or harmony. "Ye have heard that it was said, An eye for an eye, and a tooth for a tooth," but "This is my commandment, that ye love one another." So long as we have destructive thoughts, so long as we war in thought with our neighbor next door or on the other side of the earth, just so long shall we have inharmony, just so long shall we fall short of being true followers of Jesus. We must love, we must forgive, we must harmonize our thoughts under the divine law; then we shall heal and resurrect the body.

# Chapter 18

## Transfiguration

*Be ye transformed by the renewing of your mind.*

Transfiguration is always preceded by a change of mind. Our ideas must be lifted from the material, the physical, to the spiritual. But first we need to realize that it is possible for us to be transfigured as well as to understand the law by which transfiguration is brought about.

The meaning of the Transfiguration has never been understood by those who read the Scriptures as history. The transfiguration of Jesus has always been considered a historical event, and its allegorical meaning overlooked. To get the real meaning of the Transfiguration, we must regard the experience of Jesus on the mount as typical of what often takes place in those who are growing in spiritual consciousness.

We have evidences every day of the power of thought to transfigure the countenance. We know that it is possible for a person to be transformed in a degree by the thoughts that flit through his mind from moment to moment, but we do not know his capacity for transfiguration, which is unlimited, nor the part it plays in his attainment of the Christ consciousness and the Christ body.

The real object of existence is to bring forth the perfect man and attain eternal life. Eternal life must be earned. It is usually assumed that man does not die, and this is true of the I AM; but how about the consciousness, the soul? "The soul that sinneth, it shall die" is the testimony of the Scriptures. That only lives which conforms to the principle of eternal life.

Spirit exists eternally in God-Mind, of which we must become conscious. This consciousness is soul and is the tangible part of soul. God-Mind gives us the opportunity to incorporate into our consciousness His attributes. These attributes are spiritual life, love, wisdom, strength, power, in fact the essence of all good, which we realize first in mind, then in body and affairs. Thus God gives us the spiritual perfection that we are to manifest and retain eternally in consciousness. This is His Son or Christ.

Jesus taught that we must attain the consciousness of eternal life, that we have no life in us until we have attained this consciousness. Until we demonstrate over death, the death of the body, we are in a transitory state of existence.

Then the real object of existence is to attain the consciousness of eternal life and to manifest all that is potentially involved in us by our Creator. The Spirit—I AM or ego in man is eternal, but there must be a consciousness of this quality of eternity; there must be a consciousness of the image-and-likeness man. There must be in every one of us a realization of that Spirit which has in it—involved in its being—all that exists in the universal. If we do not realize this, if we do not make it ours, we must eventually go back to the universal. Jesus was the great way-shower to the attainment of this realization of Spirit, and we shall miss "the prize of the high calling" if we do not enter the path that He trod and that He pointed out in many parables, illustrations, and experiences.

Then this overcoming or lifting up of man is a process through which we are all passing if we have been converted to the Christ way of life. Transfiguration plays a part and an important part in this evolution of the soul. When we see the parallel between our experiences and the transfiguration of Jesus we gain confidence to go forward.

In our study and application of the Christian life we all have times when we are spiritually uplifted. Such a time is marked by a form of spiritual enthusiasm, which is brought about by statements of Truth made by ourselves or others—prayers, words of praise, songs, meditations—any statement of Truth that exalts the spiritual realms of the mind. Jesus was lifted up by Peter, James, and John (faith, judgment, and love). Whenever we dwell on these virtues and try to live up to them, they are exalted in consciousness, and they go up with us to the mount of Transfiguration. You may not always realize this. You may think that the uplifting was just a passing exaltation, but it stamps itself on your soul and body and marks the planting of a new idea in the upward trend of the whole man.

What is your attitude toward these times when you feel the mighty uplift of Spirit? Do you give them their due importance; or when you again come down into the valley, do you groan and question and wonder why you do not abide in your exaltation, why there seems a falling away of the mind from it?

Right here we must be wise and understand the relation of the higher principles of man and their action in the redemption of soul and body. Do not lose sight of the fact that the whole man must be spiritualized. Some people get into the habit of going up in spirit to the mount of Transfiguration, and they find it so enticing that they refuse to descend to the valley again. Then soul and body are left to go their own way, and a separation ensues. Such persons dwell continually on the heights and ignore the essential unity of Spirit, soul, and body. Many delusions arise among Christians because they lack understanding of the law of the idea and its manifestations. All things, all actions, all principles, are working toward the unity of God, man, and the universe. But there must be a readjustment and a cleansing of the whole mass. If there are things, whether mental or physical, that are not up to the high standard of Spirit, they must die. Jesus on the mount spoke of His death that was to follow. This death is of the material perception of substance and life, which is reflected in man's body of flesh. This must perish. The limited concept of matter and of a material body must be transformed so that the true spiritual body may appear.

We find that at every upward step we take in our evolution there is a sloughing off of, a doing away with, some parts of consciousness that do not accord with the higher principles. Jesus referred to it as the planting of a seed in the ground and its dying before it can bring forth the new life. The real life chit in the seed does not die. It lives and multiplies when rid of its husk of bondage. In the refinement of metals the fire, which is life, fuses the whole mass. Then the molten elements form a new base; the precious metals go by themselves and the dross goes by itself. The dross is poured off and thrown away, the precious metals are saved.

Much the same thing takes place in the action of Spirit, soul, and body when a person goes into the high consciousness and is transfigured. Some persons call it conversion, some illumination, some the lifting-up power of Spirit. Whatever you call it, it is the same thing. When the white heat of God life comes upon man, there is exaltation and transfusion of elements. The result of soul exaltation is a finer soul essence forming the base of a new body substance. The passing away of the dross of materiality is a form of death.

You have doubtless wondered: "Why is it that, after I have had an uplift, after I have had a high realization, or a strong treatment, I have to meet so many errors? It seems to me that the negative side piles in on me the next day or the next few weeks stronger than ever."

The cause of this is a gathering together of the evil and the good; the day of judgment has arrived, and you are the judge. You may even be buried for "three days" in that material consciousness which has not yet come to the full light. But when you know the law that Spirit is always with you you have nothing to fear, if you hold steadily to the Christ presence that you realized in the mount of Transfiguration.

Having once seen Truth, having once had the illumination, you find that the next step is to demonstrate it and not to be cast down or discouraged by the opposite. When the crucifixion comes and you are suffering the pangs of dying error, you may cry out, "My God, my God, why hast thou forsaken me?" forgetting for the time the promises in the mount of Transfiguration. This is when you need to realize that you are passing through a transforming process that will be followed by a resurrection of all that is worth saving.

Transfiguration is an essential step in every forward movement of men and nations. All philosophers have observed it in its various phases. Carlyle says: "Once risen into this divine white heat of temper, were it only for a season and not again, it is henceforth considerable through all its remaining history. And no nation that has not had such divine paroxysms at any time is apt to come to much."

Paul saw it in its work in man, when he wrote, "For our citizenship is in heaven; whence also we wait for a Saviour, the Lord Jesus Christ: who shall fashion anew the body of our humiliation, that it may be conformed to the body of his glory." "Then shall the righteous shine forth as the sun in the kingdom of their Father." "We know that, if he shall be manifested, we shall be like him; for we shall see him even as he is." "As we have borne the image of the earthy, we shall also bear the image of the heavenly."

It is quite essential that those who are striving for "the prize of the high calling of God in Christ Jesus" cling to their ideal as real. It should not be regarded in the light of a past event or of a future achievement, but as fulfillment here and now. This is illustrated in the communion of Moses and Elijah with Jesus on the mount, Moses representing the law, Elijah its fulfillment. Jesus is the I AM, in which both the past and the future are joined. But Peter, not understanding the lesson, wanted to make three tabernacles, representing the tendency of man to separate and localize that which is spiritual and universal.

When the voice of Principle proclaimed the spiritual man's presence—"This is my beloved Son, in whom I am well pleased; hear ye him"—there were no promises of the past or the future. Time has no power over one who dwells in the mind of God. There is no time to the mind of one who realizes omnipresence. Nothing will transfigure the race and renew the body so rapidly as the denial of both past and future. Persons get childish because they let their thoughts dwell upon the past. Fear of the future weakens the virile life, and the feet stumble. The Son of God is vigorous with the increasing life that is perpetually flowing forth from the Father. When man realizes the omnipresent life his whole organism is vitalized, and the soul is glorified. When man is in spiritual consciousness his soul shines with an energy that electrifies the outer clothing. Those little points of magnetic light, which we have all observed upon removing our clothing at night, are weak manifestations of the aura of the soul, which can be magnified until the whole body is ablaze with it.

Some Christians teach the saving of the soul and the perishing of the body. Jesus taught the saving of both soul and body. It is true that this mortal body must be transfigured; it is but a picture or symbol of the real, the spiritual body, which is the "Lord's body." The "Lord's body" is the body of Spirit, the divine idea of a perfect human body. When one realizes this new body, the cells of the present body will form on new planes of consciousness, they will aggregate around new centers, and the "Lord's body" will appear.

"But we all, with unveiled face beholding as in a mirror the glory of our Lord, are transformed into the same image from glory to glory, even as from the Lord the Spirit."

When the body is devitalized by excessive labor, dissipation, or any loss of vital force, its aura shrinks away and a consciousness akin to that of being unclothed is evident. To dream of being naked or partly clothed is a warning by Spirit that the reserve vital force has been dissipated and the natural clothing of the body removed. Continuous disregard of the law of conservation of vital force is followed by various diseases and finally death. During sleep the system, under natural law, seeks to equalize the vital forces, and it does so if the intellectual concentration has not been too great. A dream of falling means that this force, which has been piled up in the head, is falling down into the lower channels of the body, and is restoring equilibrium at the expense of harmonious reaction. When the mind is adjusted to the divine law, all the vital forces flow harmoniously and the aura glows about the body as a beautiful white light, protecting it from all discord from without and purifying it continually from within.

This is the state of the perfected man described in Revelation 1:14–16.

"And his head and his hair were white as white wool, white as snow; and his eyes were as a flame of fire; and his feet like unto burnished brass . . . and his voice as the voice of many waters. . . . and his countenance was as the sun shineth in his strength."

# Chapter 19

## The End of the Age

In all ages and among all people, there have been legends of prophets and saviors and predictions of their coming. Anticipation of a messiah has not been confined to the Occident, for several of the prominent religions of the Orient have prophesied a messiah. The fact that all who believe in the principle of divine incarnation have long strained their eyes across the shining sands in an effort to catch sight of the coming of one clothed with the power of heaven, should make us pause and consider the cause of such universality of opinion among peoples widely separated. To dismiss the subject as a religious superstition is not in harmony with unprejudiced reason. To regard these prophecies merely as religious superstitions rules out traditions that are as tenable and as reliable as the facts of history. There is a cause for every effect, and the cause underlying this almost unanimous expectation of a messiah must have some of the omnipresence of a universal law.

In considering a subject like this, which demonstrates itself largely on metaphysical lines, it is necessary to look beyond the material plane to the realm of causes.

The material universe is but the shadow of the spiritual universe. The pulsations of the spiritual forces impinge upon and sway men, nations, and planets, according to laws whose sweep in space and time is so stupendous as to be beyond the ken or comprehension of astronomy. But the fact should not be overlooked that higher astronomy had its votaries in the past. The Magi and the illumined sages of Chaldea and Egypt had astronomical knowledge of universal scope. It was so broad, so gigantic, so far removed from the comprehension of the common mind of their day that it always remained the property of the few. It was communicated in symbols, because of the poverty of language to express its supermundane truths. In the sacred literature of the Hindus are evidences of astronomical erudition covering such vast periods of time that modern philosophers cannot or do not give them credence, and they are relegated to the domain of speculation rather than of science. However the astronomers of the present age have forged along on material lines until now they are beginning to impinge upon the hidden wisdom of the mighty savants of the past.

There is evidence that proves that the ages of the distant past knew a higher astronomy than do we of this age, and that they predicted the future of this planet through cycles and aeons—its nights of mental darkness and the dawn of its spiritual day—with the same accuracy that our astronomers do its present-day planetary revolutions.

Jesus evidently understood this higher astronomy, and He knew that His work as a teacher and demonstrator of spiritual law was related to it, yet not controlled by it. He co-operated with the "law . . . and the prophets," as far as they went, but He knew the higher law of the Christ man and affirmed His supremacy in the words: "All authority hath been given unto me in heaven and on earth."

Jesus evidently understood the aeons or ages through which the earth passes. For example, in Matthew 13:39, our English Bible reads: "The enemy that sowed them is the devil: and the harvest is the end of the world; and the reapers are angels." In the Diaglott version, which gives the original Greek and a word-for-word translation, this reads: "THAT ENEMY who SOWED them is the ADVERSARY; the HARVEST is the End of the Age; and the REAPERS are Messengers." In this as in many other passages where Jesus used the word "age," it has been translated "world," leading the reader to believe that Jesus taught that this planet was to be destroyed.

So we see that the almost universally accepted teaching of the end of the world is not properly founded on the Bible. The translators wanted to give the wicked a great scare, so they put "the end of the world" into Jesus' mouth in several instances where He plainly said "the end of the age."

The Bible is a textbook of absolute Truth; but its teachings are veiled in symbol and understood only by the illumined. The old prophets knew that the earth would become spiritualized in time, and they looked forward and saw it as a self-luminous planet. This is plainly stated in numerous places in the Scriptures. Isaiah says: "Arise, shine; for thy light is come, and the glory of Jehovah is risen upon thee. . . . Violence shall no more be heard in thy land, desolation nor destruction within thy borders . . . The sun shall be no more thy light by day; neither for brightness shall the moon give light unto thee: but Jehovah will be unto thee an everlasting light, and thy God thy glory." John in Revelation also saw a like condition when he prophesied: "And there shall be night no more; and they need no light of lamp, neither light of sun; for the Lord God shall give them light."

Job wrote:

> "*Canst thou lead forth the Mazzaroth ['the signs of the Zodiac' (margin)] in their season? . . .*
> *Knowest thou the ordinances of the heavens?*
> *Canst thou establish the dominion thereof in the earth?*"

In accordance with the prophecies of the ancients, our planetary system has just completed a journey of 2,169 years, in which there has been wonderful material progress without its spiritual counterpart. But old conditions have passed away and a new era has dawned. A great change is taking place in the mentality of the race, and this change is evidenced in literature, science, and religion. There is a breaking away from old creeds and old doctrines, and there is a tendency to form centers along lines of scientific spiritual thought. The literature of the first half of the twentieth century is so saturated with occultism as to be an object of censure by conservatives, who denounce it as a "lapse into the superstition of the past." Notwithstanding the protests of the conservatives, on every hand are evidences of spiritual freedom; it crops out in so many ways that an enumeration would cover the whole field of life.

This is surely the coming of the spirit of Christ or Truth, just as was prophesied: "For yourselves know perfectly that the day of the Lord so cometh as a thief in the night." "And it shall come to pass afterward, that I will pour out my Spirit upon all flesh; and your sons and your daughters shall prophesy, your old men shall dream dreams, your young men shall see visions."

It is evident that Jesus and His predecessors had knowledge of coming events on lines of such absolute accuracy as to place it in the realm of truth ascertained, that is, exact science.

That knowledge of our planet is daily becoming more refined, is admitted by material scientists, but that it will ever become spiritualized, as was declared by the ancients, they do not yet admit.

The evidences of a radiant condition of matter on our planet, are so plain that even the most skeptical are loath to deny them, and they must eventually be accepted by all scientists. The physicists are rapidly altering their viewpoint. They are working out their researches in the mental realm. Recently one of the greatest of them, Professor Robert Andrews Millikan, wrote that "matter is no longer a mere game of marbles played by blind men. An atom is now an amazingly complicated organism, possessing many interrelated parts and exhibiting many functions and properties—energy properties, radiation properties, wave properties, and other properties, quite as mysterious as any that used to masquerade under the name of 'mind.' Hence the phrase 'All is matter' and 'All is mind' have now become mere shibboleths completely devoid of meaning."

But these material evidences of a new era are not necessary to the sensitive ones who feel it in the very atmosphere and who are thrilled by the light of the Christ principle. To those who hunger after righteousness, this Christ principle is the elixir of eternal life; but those who are wedded to things material would better beware! The race is changing its vibrations to a higher rate, and the higher types of the race must keep the equipoise by unfolding spiritually or they will lose their hold. Cases of loss of mental poise are now getting so numerous as to attract the attention of the medical world, and these cases will increase in frequency in the future, unless there is a stronger development of the spiritual nature of men. Old things are passing away!

Do you belong to the old, or are you building anew from within and keeping time with the progress of the age? The "harvest" or "consummation of the age" pointed out by Jesus is not far off. This is no theological scare; it is a statement based on a law that is now being tested and proved.

Listen to your inner voice; cultivate the good, the pure, the God within you. Do not let your false beliefs keep you in the darkness of error until you go out like a dying ember. The divine spark is within you. Fan it into flame by right thinking, right living, and right doing, and you will find the "new Jerusalem."

That Jesus was the fulfillment in the flesh of the long-looked-for Messiah is accepted by those who have had spiritual illumination, and is believed by millions who have not had this illumination. Many have not lifted up the Son of man in themselves, but they have faith that Jesus did. Those who study the life of Jesus in its personal aspect, to the exclusion of the spiritual, sense the wonderful possibilities within man and the universe. One who does not develop his own spiritual nature cannot see the spiritual nature in Jesus or in other men who are following Jesus in the regeneration.

Man employs a divine-natural law of growth or evolution before he reaches the divine spiritual. Those under the divine-natural law are referred to in the Bible as the "children of God." However it is possible for the "children of God" to forge ahead of the average in spiritual understanding and power, and to become those who are called "sons of God." All great spiritual leaders have been of the latter class. They see that

> "The fault . . . is not in our stars,
> But in ourselves, that we are underlings."

What we all need is a fuller understanding of the spiritual laws lying back of the phenomena of existence. "It is the spirit that giveth life; the flesh profiteth nothing." Christians should seek the undying life and law of

Jesus and the creative substance of His body instead of the historical man of Nazareth. Abstract Truth is good as a beginning for the aspiring man, but Truth incarnated through a great One is a dynamic booster, and we all intuitively unite with such a one as Jesus, and are set free from our human limitations by the vision and quickening that contact with the Christ gives us.

It is a strange fact that in attempts to get the world's estimate of great men the name of Jesus has seldom been suggested. One would think that the army of men and women teaching the doctrines of this greatest of men, would put His name at the head of the list. Our attention is always called to the classifications "secular" and "religious" to explain why Jesus is not included among the world's great men. In fact, Jesus is not considered a man but a god, and in this fact we find another of the many separations that systematized religion has made between the spiritual and the material.

The secular world has been taught that Jesus was so superior to mortal man that He can be thought of only as a god. This removes Him from us all as a man whose character we may emulate and as an example of what we may become and places His attainments far beyond human possibilities.

But Jesus laid no claim to that superiority over other men with which the church so persistently invests Him. His teaching is that all who keep the divine law as He kept it will become like Him and His disciples. "Neither for these only do I pray, but for them also that believe on me through their word." "I in them, and thou in me, that they may be perfected into one; that the world may know that thou didst send me, and lovedst them, even as thou lovedst me."

By separating Jesus from the rest of the race we close the door against the real man, the man that every personal man must progress into. "My little children, of whom I am again in travail until Christ be formed in you," said Paul. There is a great awakening, in all parts of the world, to the absolute necessity and immediate possibility of a race of men patterned after Jesus of Nazareth. Thus is germinating the seed of the new race that Jesus sowed. "Except a grain of wheat fall into the earth and die, it abideth by itself alone; but if it die, it beareth much fruit." Jesus taught the highest Truth ever given to the world, but in addition to His doctrines He gave the race His purified, glorified body. He purified and spiritualized the natural blood until it became a spiritual life stream, into which all may enter and be cleansed. He spiritualized the cells of His corruptible body and set them free in "the heavens," where we may all appropriate or "eat" them. The heavenly kingdom to which Jesus so often referred is the unlimited spiritual consciousness where mind and body are equal in all activities. When we come into the full consciousness of "the heavens," the body will respond instantly to every thought; then time, space, and all the limitations of matter will disappear. It is in this consciousness that Jesus now lives; His "second coming" will be the revealing to men and women everywhere that He has not been absent at any time. "Lo, I am with you always."

The heavenly signs of the second coming of the Son of man are in the cosmic ether, which is now known to science as interpenetrating all things. In the invisible ether, we shall eventually find a complete record of the history of the race, which spiritually developed man will be able to read as easily as he now reads the daily paper. Sir James Jeans in his book "The Mysterious Universe" says: "We must think of space as being drenched with almost all the cosmic radiation which has ever been generated since the world began. Its rays come to us as messengers not only from the farthest depths of space, but also from the farthest reaches of time. And, if we read it aright, their message seems to be that somewhere, sometime, in the history of the universe, matter has been annihilated, and this not in tiny, but in stupendous amounts."

Jesus named God-Mind the "KINGDOM of the HEAVENS." According to the original Greek, as given in the Emphatic Diaglott, He said: "Reform! because the ROYAL MAJESTY of the HEAVENS has approached." Bible translators have not understood the spiritual meaning of the Scriptures, and they have nearly always translated the word "heavens" in the singular, making it read "heaven." This error has misled many into thinking that Jesus, in His many parables and comparisons, referred to a place called heaven. But it is apparent that in these parables and comparisons He was trying to explain to His hearers the character of the omnipresent substance and life that has all potentiality and is the source of everything that appears on the earth.

The coming in the clouds of the heavens of the "Son of man sitting at the right hand of Power," as Jesus told the high priest, is the "second coming," and we should look nowhere else for the advent of the risen Christ. Christ is today "sitting at the right hand of Power," which represents spiritual power expressed; the clouds of heaven being the obscurity in which sense consciousness holds the light of Truth.

Let us cease expecting Christ to come in bodily form; let us turn our attention to His risen body already with us. In this way we shall co-operate with Him in setting up the kingdom of the heavens on the earth. In Matthew 24-23-27 Jesus gave the strongest kind of warning against the idea of the personal appearance of the Christ. This passage concludes with these words: "For as the lightning cometh forth from the east, and is seen even unto the west; so shall be the coming of the Son of man." These are Jesus' own words, and they should have greater weight than Paul's theory that Jesus will appear with a great shout in the clouds of heaven, which has been interpreted literally as the personal appearance of Jesus in the sky.

The world needs the Christ consciousness. The need implies that the attainment is near at hand. There are men and women who gaze up into the heavens for Christ, as did the early disciples, instead of looking within their own heart and mind. "Ye men of Galilee, why stand ye looking into heaven?" Only believe in the omnipresent Christ and you will behold Him sitting on the right hand of Power within your own being!

All who believe that Christ is here now should teach it and preach it with all possible zeal.

The people are longing and reaching out for the healing hand of the Lord Jesus Christ.

There is great need of leadership under the Christ whose banner is love.

The Prince of Peace should be invited to the peace conferences that are held by war-taxed and war-weary peoples.

Christ righteousness should be dominant in settling the differences between capital and labor.

Our schools in every grade need to teach the moral standard of Christ as fundamental to all true character.

When our children have the Christ Spirit pointed out to them as being within and as a living fount of health, wealth, and happiness, they will quickly accept it.

Then the ambition of men will be to compete in bringing forth Truth, goodness, and righteousness; and evil and sin, with its sickness and poverty, will disappear from the earth.

# Question Helps

**Chapter 1**
## The Atomic Age

1. What great truth have our scientists revealed to man by breaking into the atom? Tell in your own words how both Elijah and Jesus used the same energy that was discovered by them.

2. Did Jesus claim to have the exclusive supernatural power that is usually credited to Him? Explain.

3. To what is the revival of the divine law of healing due? How may the sick be restored to life and health?

4. What have thought concentration and discovery of the dynamic character of the atom to do with prayer? Explain.

5. Of what is the six-day creation of the universe (described in Genesis) a story? Explain how the privileges of the superrealm are open to all.

6. What will be the next great achievement of science?

7. How is man to achieve immortal life?

8. What part does faith play in the transformation of man?

9. What does the latest discovery of science reveal? Explain fully.

10. What must come about before mankind can truly receive the beneficial and permanent uplift to be wrought by atomic energy?

## Chapter 2
## The Restorative Power of the Spirit

1. Explain the spiritual import of Jesus' words "My Father worketh even until now, and I work."

2. What is the meaning of "I will be what I will be"?

3. In what sense is every man a king?

4. How does man's belief in his own inefficiency hinder his spiritual progress?

5. Why is a vegetarian diet inducive to a high state of spiritual unfoldment?

6. How does man become conscious of the guidance of Spirit?

7. It is possible for us to develop a radiant body temple?

8. In what state of existence is Jesus manifesting Himself today?

9. How does man save himself form unpleasant psychic or "spooky" experiences in the process of transmuting his body from the physical to the supersubstance state?

10. Give in your own words Charles Fillmore's account of the development of the radiant body within himself.

## Chapter 3
## Spiritual Obedience

1. What is spiritual zeal?
2. While on his way to Damascus to persecute the Christians the zealous Saul's concept of religion went through a complete change. Explain fully.
3. Why should zeal be tempered with wisdom?
4. Why should man be obedient to Spirit? Explain.
5. Above all other Bible writers what important point did Paul emphasize?
6. What does prayer do for man?
7. Explain the outpouring of the dynamic power of Spirit as recorded in Acts 1 and 2.
8. Jesus said that he was the bread and substance that came down from heaven. When will our civilization begin to realize and appropriate this boundless substance and life?
9. What is the dominion that God gave man in the beginning? Explain.
10. In the economy of the future what will take place?

## Chapter 4
## I AM or Superconsciousness

1. Define superconsciousness.
2. Explain how Jesus externalized the superconsciousness, thus making it an abiding place for the race.
3. Explain the method by which Jesus evolved from sense to God consciousness.

4. How does man overcome all error beliefs?

5. Explain how the mind of man is built on Truth.

6. What great truth did Jesus prove by His resurrection and ascension?

7. What accomplishments are possible to man through the Holy Spirit?

8. Modern science reveals that imprisoned within the cells of man's body are electronic energies beyond possibility of estimate. Of what practical use is this knowledge to man today?

9. Can man free himself and others from the claim of materiality? Explain.

10. How is man loosed from all limiting thoughts and set free in the Christ consciousness.

## Chapter 5
The Day of Judgment

1. Define the term "Son of man."

2. When do we begin to pass judgment? Explain.

3. How do we separate our good thoughts from thoughts of disease, death, lack, and the like?

4. How do we handle our "goat" thoughts?

5. At what stage of unfoldment do we begin to have fine, discriminating judgment?

6. "Then shall the King say unto them on the right hand, Come, ye blessed of my Father, inherit the kingdom prepared for you from the foundation of the world." Who is the King? Explain.

7. How do we reap the benefit of all the good we have ever done or thought?

8. When is everything in Principle ours?

9. Explain how the body becomes full of light.

10. In this connection what is the work of the I AM?

**Chapter 6**
## Thou Shalt Decree a Thing

1. How does man fix an ideal in substance?

2. Define "the visible."

3. Since nothing is really lost, what becomes of the energy that is being released in the disintegration that is going on in the earth?

4. How may man develop a purer, sweeter body and a saner mind?

5. Explain how the destiny of the race is in the hands of man.

6. What will save the race from being destroyed?

7. Name at least three instances in the Bible where marvelous results followed the blowing of trumpets used in the observance of religious rites.

8. Explain how these results were accomplished.

9. How does the trained metaphysician produce like results?

10. Explain how faith plays an important part in broadcasting messages of light to receptive minds.

**Chapter 7**
## Thinking in the Fourth Dimension

1. Do the stupendous truths science is discovering today parallel the truths of the invisible side of life that Jesus taught? Explain.

2. It is necessary for man in the present day to develop a capacity for understanding in terms of the atomic structure of the universe? Give reasons for your answer.

3. Define Jesus' words "If any man hath ears to hear, let him hear."

4. In developing the inner ear we sometimes hear deceptive voices. How may this situation be handled scientifically?

5. Give your interpretation of these words of Jesus: "For unto every one that hath shall be given, and he shall have abundance: but from him that hath not, even that which he hath shall be taken away."

6. Should the discoveries of science be divorced from the kingdom of the heavens taught by Jesus? Explain.

7. Are the mysteries of the supermind open to all alike? What is the result?

8. Does man have power to dominate nature? Explain.

9. What is the great need of the whole human family?

10. Explain the need for a larger realization of the importance of man in manifesting God.

## Chapter 8
Is This God's World?

1. Is God responsible for all that occurs on this earth, and if not, how much?

2. "Thou makest him [man] to have dominion over the works of thy hands: Thou hast put all things under his feet." Explain the significance of these words of the Psalmist in relation to the atomic bomb.

3. Eventually how may our standard of living be vastly improved by the utilization of atomic forces?

4. Is it necessary today to give more attention to the refinement of the body temple?

5. Explain the difference between a prayer treatment given by an experienced spiritual healer and the shocks given by mechanical generators.

6. Is this God's world? Give reasons for your answer.

7. Is it possible to determine how many ages have passed since man lost contact with God? Explain.

8. Where is man's home?

9. What is the great and important issue before the people today?

10. What is the one and only way out of the chaos?

## Chapter 9
## Demonstrating Christ Thought by Thought

1. What great truth do the "signs of the times" reveal?

2. How can fear and worry and other limitations be overcome?

3. How can we demonstrate a well body?

4. What is the one way to establish harmony in the home?

5. Explain why we should yield obediently to the transforming process of Spirit.

6. What parts do imagination and faith play in demonstration?

7. Is it necessary to live the Truth in order to demonstrate it? Explain.

8. Is there anything mysterious in being led by Spirit? Explain.

9. How are errors in the subconscious mind eliminated?

10. Define the phrase "body of Christ" in its threefold significance.


**Chapter 10**
Truth Radiates Light

1. Define body temple and explain what is necessary in order to glorify the body.

2. In Exodus we read, "Let them make me a sanctuary, that I may dwell among them." Give the metaphysical meaning of this Scripture.

3. What does it mean to burn incense in the house of Jehovah?

4. What is the result when our mind is lifted up in prayer?

5. The Israelites did not go forward in the wilderness on days when the cloud remained over the Tabernacle but only when the cloud was lifted. Give the metaphysical meaning of this.

6. What is the first step in getting out of a mental cloud?

7. When Moses came down from Mount Sinai with the Ten Commandments his countenance shone so brilliantly they had to put a veil over his face. Explain from a scientific viewpoint.

8. What effect do fervent words expressed in eloquent proclamations of spiritual Truth have upon man?

9. Do you consider the tendency on the part of metaphysicians to analyze scientifically these experiences sacrilegious? Give reason for your answer.

10. When the student searches for the science in religion and the religion in science what does he discover? Please amplify.

## Chapter 11
## The Only Mind

1. Explain in your own language where ideas come from and in what realm they operate.

2. Can man analyze mind and understand its laws and modes of operation? Give reason for your answer.

3. On what plane alone can we know Truth in an absolute sense? Explain.

4. What relation do language and formulation bear to mind?

5. Explain the difference between intellectual knowledge and pure spiritual knowing.

6. Regardless of lack of technical education, what results when man gives his mind to the attention of the one Mind?

7. What is the great difference between what the physical scientist calls "universal energy" and the metaphysician calls God-Mind?

8. Explain how man is a co-creator with God.

9. When man seeks the Father with an eye single to His guidance what is the result?

10. What is man's first step after he has learned spiritual obedience?

**Chapter 12**

Contact with the Christ Mind

1.  Is man consciously in intimate contact with the Holy Spirit? How may an understanding of Holy Spirit activity strengthen man's faith?

2.  What is the meaning of the name El Shaddai?

3.  Explain how the Holy Spirit in Divine Mind corresponds to man's thought in his mind.

4.  How may we approach God with confidence; and what is the result?

5.  Explain in your own words the relation of the universal or Jehovah-Mind to the personal or Christ Mind.

6.  How may we get into conscious contact with the Christ Mind and demonstrate over sin, sickness, and death? Explain fully.

7.  Jesus taught that the true way to demonstrate abundance is to be "rich toward God." Explain in your own words how this sure law of demonstration operates.

8.  Why should human egotism be repressed? Explain fully.

9.  How can man greatly accelerate the formation in him of the Christ Mind?

10. Give fully the origin of anger, revenge, fear, poverty, failure, and the like, and explain how these error conditions can be changed into love, courage, peace, prosperity, and success.

## Chapter 13
## Metaphysics of Shakespeare

1. Give in your own words an estimate of the true character of Shakespeare.

2. What do Shakespeare's writings reveal as regards his spiritual understanding?

3. Where would you look for the antecedents of Shakespeare? Give reasons for your answer.

4. Every soul has an untapped mine of knowledge in the subconscious mind, inspiration and rediscovery being the positive and negative poles of the mind. What was the relation of Shakespeare's thought to these sources of knowledge? Explain.

5. In Shakespeare's play "Julius Caesar" what is revealed by the two different interpretations of Calpurnia's dream?

6. In "Hamlet" Hamlet's father's ghost appears and gives a Graphic description of how he had been murdered by the king. What does this reveal as to Shakespeare's thought?

7. Shakespeare did not teach religion but the facts of life as he saw them. Explain.

8. Although Shakespeare may not have applied the law of spiritual healing to himself, is there evidence that he perceived the possibility of such healing? Give reasons for your answer.

9. While Shakespeare was familiar with the superstitions of his age, did he usually point out the fallacies in them? Explain.

10. Does the genius displayed in Shakespeare's writings belong wholly to the men and women of his time or to all generations? Give reasons for your answer.

## Chapter 14
### The Body

1. Define the Bible in terms of the subject presented in this chapter.

2. What is the paramount theme of the New Testament and in fact the veiled theme of the entire Bible?

3. According to the explanation given in this chapter, what is man? Does man really despise his body? Explain.

4. What is the body?

5. Is the belief that the resurrection of the body has to do with the getting of a new body after death founded on the principles of Truth? Give reasons for your answer.

6. Give explanation of Paul's words "When this corruptible shall have put on incorruption, and this mortal shall have put on immortality . . . Death is swallowed up in victory."

7. How may men become a Christ in mind and in body?

8. Explain in your own words how a pattern of the perfect body is stamped in every soul and how this pattern may be brought into manifestation.

9. Explain how Jesus, who overcame death even in the body, is our normal standard.

10. How do we establish our ego, our I AM identity with Divine Mind, and step by step eliminate the old and put on the new?

## Chapter 15
## Faith Precipitations

1. Compare the way electricity operates on the physical plane with the way faith operates in the realm of mind.

2. Did Jesus require co-operation in faith on the part of those He healed in order to complete the healing circuit? Why is this necessary?

3. (a) When are speedy answers to prayer experienced?
   (b) With whom does the fulfillment of the law rest?

4. (a) Did Jesus teach persistence in prayer? Explain.
   (b) What is the teaching of Jesus about God's being the law as well as the Spirit?

5. Explain how ephemeral Caesars become world leaders Today. Explain fully.

6. If the supermind ability is in every man, why is it not more widely understood and used?

7. When and how was the hypnotic spell of ecclesiastical authority broken, and how long was it in abeyance? Explain.

8. Explain in your own words the reformation of which we have today seen only the beginning.

9. Did Jesus teach the immortality of the body as well as of the soul? Explain.

10. Are there any incurable diseases? Explain fully.

## Chapter 16
## The Seed Is the Word

1. In your own words explain Being in its twofold aspect.
2. What is the word of God?
3. Do "things" have causative power? Explain.
4. Define man and explain how he draws his substance from the infinite storehouse.
5. Give the metaphysical meaning of the statement "I am the door."
6. When man ceases to remember the source of his being what Is the result?
7. Interpret Jesus' words "Man shall not live by bread alone, but by every word that proceedeth out of the mouth of God."
8. Is there any evidence that man is a miraculous creation? Explain.
9. Explain in your own words the statement that every idea is a seed and brings forth according to its character.
10. Man's mind is a garden, where he is in control and himself determines just what kind of seed words are to grow there. Elaborate.

## Chapter 17
## The Resurrecting Power of the Word

1. Jesus Christ is the fulfillment of the promise. "As in Adam all die, so also in Christ shall all be made alive." Explain.

2. Why is it difficult for man to realize that he can overcome the negative conditions called sickness and death?

3. What unalterable truth does the Easter lesson reveal to us?

4. When Jesus received His illumination and stepped forth as a teacher did He meet with any opposition? Explain.

5. If a demonstration of resurrection were to take place today, what would be the attitude of men in general?

6. Explain the difference between the astral or ghostly body of the dead and the resurrected body of Jesus.

7. How may we come into eternal life and save the body from the disintegrating effects of death?

8. What has right thinking to do with making the demonstration of eternal life? Explain.

9. (a) What are the two activities of the word mentioned in this chapter?

   (b) What determines the measure of power possessed by our words?

10. Explain in your own language the meaning of the Scripture "If a man keep my word, he shall never taste of death."

## Chapter 18
Transfiguration

1. What does the word "transfiguration" mean to you?

2. Do those who read the Scriptures merely as history understand the true meaning of "transfiguration"? Explain.

3. What is the real object of existence?

4. Explain how Jesus was lifted up on the mount of Transfiguration and how man may also be lifted up.

5. What is the result when one tries to live continually in the high state of realization and neglects to lift up soul and body?

6. On the mount Jesus spoke of His death which was to follow. Explain and give illustration.

7. Why is it that after the uplift that follows a strong spiritual realization one has to meet seeming errors of various kinds?

8. Is transfiguration as essential step in every forward movement of men and nations? Give reasons for your answer.

9. Has time any power over one who dwells in the mind of God? Explain fully.

10. (a)What does it mean when one dreams of being naked or partly clothed?

    (b) What happens when the mind is adjusted to the divine law?

## Chapter 19
## The End Of The Age

1. Throughout the ages all nations and all peoples have been looking for the coming of One clothed with the power of heaven. Explain this idea from a metaphysical standpoint.

2. Did Jesus understand the higher astronomy of past ages? What was his attitude toward it?

3. Is the accepted teaching of "the end of the world" founded on the Bible? Explain.

4. As the mentality of the race changes as evidenced in literature, science, and religion is there a corresponding growth in spiritual freedom? Give full explanation.

5. Explain how to hold fast to the Christ principles in order to retain mental balance during the present time, in which the race is changing its vibrations to a higher rate.

6. Who are the "children of God"? Who are the "sons of God"?

7. How do we enter into a fuller understanding of the spiritual laws lying back of the phenomena of existence?

8. Explain fully why we should not separate Jesus from the rest of the race but should look upon Him as our way-shower.

9. Give a scientific explanation of the second coming of the Son of man. Give reasons for your answer.

10. What does the great need in the world today of the Christ consciousness imply? Give reasons for your answer.